More than Meets the Eye

A NEW LOOK AT FLOWER ARRANGING

More than Meets the Eye

A NEW LOOK AT FLOWER ARRANGING

Sue Phillips

Stanley Paul

London Melbourne Auckland Johannesburg

First published in 1986 by Stanley Paul
an imprint of Century Hutchinson Ltd,
Brookmount House, 62–65 Chandos Place,
Covent Garden, London WC2N 4NW

Century Hutchinson Publishing Group
(Australia) Pty Ltd
16–22 Church Street, Hawthorn, Melbourne,
Victoria 3122

Century Hutchinson Group (NZ) Ltd
32–34 View Road, PO Box 40–086, Glenfield,
Auckland 10

Century Hutchinson Group (SA) Pty Ltd
PO Box 337, Bergvlei 2012, South Africa

Set in Palatino by
The Castlefield Press, Moulton, Northampton
Printed and bound in Great Britain by
Butler and Tanner Ltd, Frome and London

ISBN 0 09 162551 3

Contents

Acknowledgements

I'd like to take this opportunity to thank all the people who have been, in any way, connected with the television series More Than Meets The Eye, without which there would have been no book to base on it.

But particular thanks are due to John Wareing, Elizabeth Palmer, and Maureen Foster who kindly wrote sections on their particular specialities in flower arranging for this book. John, and Maureen's husband Barry, also contributed their own line drawings and photographs as well. I am grateful too to The Flower Council of Holland, the Floristry Section at the College of Further Education in Plymouth, Interflora, Joan Lutwyche, and the Royal Horticultural Society – all of whom have generously helped with photography.

The flower arrangements you are about to see have been created by John and Bett Wareing, Lizanne Weston, Michael Saunders, Takashi Sawano, Tinneka Robertson, Pamela South, Maureen Foster, Kenneth Turner, and Bridget Stanley.

A special thank-you to Alan Mole, Tessa and Sarah at the Flower Council of Holland for all their help this side of the water, and to Warren for negociating the language problems the other side.

And finally, my thanks to Television South West for all their exceptional patience, professionalism and hard work in making the series – Derek, Karen, Tom, the make-up ladies, 'wardrobe', and the crew.

SUE PHILLIPS

Introduction

Flower arranging is one of those things you can't do unless you're an expert – and you can't become an expert until you can do it, or so the story goes. But it's a lot of nonsense.

One thing is certain: flowers really do make your home a more attractive place to live in. And whether you call yourself a 'flower arranger' or not, there's no reason why you shouldn't be perfectly able to use flowers to do just that. Forget about the 'rules' that the muck-and-mystery brigade would have you believe are essential. There is no right or wrong way to arrange flowers. At the end of the day, if you are satisfied with the result it must be right. Even if you don't think of yourself as artistic you can still work wonders with flowers just by having some good ideas to work from, and by not being afraid to have a go.

This book, based on the Television South West series *More Than Meets the Eye*, isn't a flower arranging manual. Instead it shows that there is more than one way of arranging flowers – if the regulation 'triangles' don't appeal to you there are plenty of other interesting ways of handling them – and it gives an idea of the background to something that most of us take for granted. And even if all you've done in the way of arranging so far is sticking a bunch of daffs into a milk bottle, you'll find enough of the basics to get you started.

But be warned. Once you've caught the bug, you'll soon find that you can't do without flowers.

1 The English Style

We English are known all over the world for being just a little bit daft about gardens, particularly when it comes to flowers. And it seems we just can't get enough of a good thing. Whether it is due to our unpredictable weather, which all too often prevents us looking at flowers out of doors, I don't know. But one thing is for sure – we can't just leave them in the garden. They have worked their way, not only indoors, but into the very fabric of the English way of life. Flowers are all around us.

Just take a look round your living room. Even if you don't have the real thing in a vase or a pot on your windowsill, you will probably have some flower designs: flowers on the wallpaper, curtains, chair covers, carpets, in pictures, on the tea service . . . the list is endless. And even if you don't happen to think of yourself as a gardener or a flower arranger, flowers probably play a much more important part in your life than you realize. For instance, can you imagine a wedding without flowers?

Flowers as part of the English tradition

The custom linking flowers and weddings goes back so far that no one really knows when it began, or why. But there is a lot of folklore behind it, and people still say that whoever catches the bride's bouquet will be the next to get married.

Today's fashionable wedding bouquets often contain carnations or roses, but traditionally myrtle was the essential wedding flower. After the wedding was over, the chief bridesmaid would plant a shoot of myrtle from the bride's bouquet next to the door of the couple's new home. When the young plant flowered, another wedding was foretold – this time, the bridesmaid's. It was unfortunate if the bridesmaid was not much of a gardener: if her cutting died, she could only

A typically English
wedding: the bride
carries a traditional
bouquet of fresh
flowers. She wears too
a circlet of flowers on
her head, and her
bridegroom sports the
classic English
buttonhole, a rose

expect to be an old maid. Over a century after Queen Victoria's
wedding, myrtle grown from her bouquet was used in
Princess Anne's, suggesting that she followed a long line of
happily married bridesmaids with green fingers.

Over the years white roses, lilies of the valley, orchids, white
violets, stephanotis and orange blossom have all been
favourites for wedding bouquets. But there are other flowers
without which the occasion is not complete. Buttonholes are a
very necessary part of the uniform of the properly turned out
bridegroom, best man and father of the bride. And no self-
respecting bride's mother would think herself properly
dressed without a corsage – often orchids these days. The
tradition springs from the Middle Ages when people needed
to carry flowers in the smelly street as a nosegay – a sort of
portable floral air freshener.

Flowers have played a role in many British traditions. For
instance, they were an important part of the May Day
celebrations. In former times this was a more boisterous
occasion. The young men of the village would rise at dawn to
gather tree branches for decoration. They would make
garlands for the oxen and place them carefully on the tips of
their horns. Suitably embellished, the oxen were led out into
the woodland where one of the trees was chosen to become the
maypole; it was cut down and brought back behind the oxen,
followed by the women and children. Stripes would be
painted on it and it would then be covered with flowers and
herbs, ready for dancing around.

The whole performance honoured the pagan god of fertility.
It all stemmed from the ancient Roman festival of Floralia,

dedicated to Flora, the goddess of flowering plants. This festival began in about 300 BC, after storms had ravaged the spring crops and it was generally felt that a little divine intervention would not go amiss. On being imported to Britain, it became loosely translated into our typical May Day celebrations which continued to follow the original pagan formula until the authorities decided it was not suitable for a Christian society, and an Act of Parliament forebade maypoles.

Throughout history, flowers have appeared on heraldic shields, along with unicorns, griffons and other emblems. Madonna lilies, burdock and broom all figure in coats of arms. So do cloves, which are the dried buds of a tropical flower and were important in the spice trade; they are the symbol of the Worshipful Company of Grocers. The Corporation of Dundee have a lily pot argent in their coat of arms. Someone else has a tasteful arrangement of pineapples. And everyone knows that the thistle is the emblem of Scotland.

One of the best-known heraldic flowers is the fleur-de-lys. If you look closely, you will see that it is actually an iris, and the story of how it came to be adopted as one of the heraldic emblems is in keeping with the best of traditions. Back in the sixth century, Clovis, King of the Franks, together with what was left of his troops, was making a strategic withdrawal after a particularly disastrous battle. As they retreated towards a river, Clovis saw irises growing in it. He realized because of this that the water was shallow enough to cross in safety. Since it had saved him and his army, he made the flower his personal emblem. Years later it was taken as the royal emblem of Louis VII of France, who called it fleur-de-Louis, which in time became corrupted to fleur-de-lys. In the fourteenth century, when Edward III of England claimed the French throne, he also acquired the fleur-de-lys, and so it became part of the English royal coat of arms. Heraldic flowers have had many historical associations; the red rose of Lancaster and the white rose of York have even had a civil war named after them – the Wars of the Roses.

Flowers as a design motif

Over the centuries, artists and designers have frequently used flowers as a decorative motif. Some of the most memorable – and often collectable – designs are flower-inspired. In fact, floral patterns have rarely been out of fashion. You only need to look at William Morris prints to see what I mean. His wallpaper and fabric designs based on flowers were popular in his day among people of taste, and have recently experienced a revival. The Victorians used flowers everywhere: on their curtains and carpets, up the wall, on footstools and firescreens and in chandeliers. And since no self-respecting middle-class parlour of the time was adequately furnished while there was a spare inch of flat surface anywhere, they also made artificial flowers of wax or feathers and covered them with glass domes. These competed for attention with the stuffed birds, petrified lizards, aspidistras and other knick-knacks that cluttered up a Victorian parlour. And just in case flowers should, even for a second, vanish from sight, the ever-thoughtful Victorians even went so far as to manufacture flower-painted lavatories.

Tiffany lamps in the form of flowers became world-famous – nowadays they are collectors' pieces worth a small fortune, which you would be jolly lucky to find turning up at the church jumble. Over the years porcelain manufacturers such as Royal Worcester have based some of their most famous designs on flowers, and flower patterns are still top sellers today.

In modern interior decoration, Sandersons have floral wallpapers and Laura Ashley has created a complete lifestyle based on flowers: flowery bedrooms, bathrooms and flowery living rooms, and of course flowery clothes.

In the sixties, hippies turned to flower power for peace. They wore flowery kaftans, gave each other flowers, and even smoked flowers – cannabis, which ironically used to be grown as a bedding plant by the Victorians. Ageing hippies in executive positions, rebelling against the white collar and conservative tie of their 'respectable' jobs, even brought flower power into the Swinging Sixties office by sporting some of the loudest of men's fashions seen since the days of the Regency bucks. Floral fashions for men came 'in' with gaudily flowered shirts and ties, causing a positive stampede into the numerous trendy boutiques that sprang up overnight to satisfy the demand for the new look.

Flowery clothes are in fact not particularly new. Throughout the history of costume, flowers have regularly been in fashion. Many collections of historical clothes contain examples of how flower patterns have persuaded the fashion-conscious to part with their money. Some of the more exaggerated dress styles, all bustle, bodice and floral embroidery, turned the wearer into a moving herbaceous border. The Victoria and Albert Museum has a particularly good collection of floral fashions in its costume collection, which includes some very spectacular hats.

Until Princess Diana brought hats back into vogue, they had been rather out of favour. But hats still feature regularly every year on the nine o' clock news – during Ascot Week when they are a high spot of the Royal racing scene. One of the most outrageous ever featured was a gigantic daisy, with petals drooping artistically around the face. Yet, whatever direction high fashion takes in hats or in anything else it remains true that the most elegant and most wearable *chapeaux* are still the broad-brimmed curving straw creations festooned with flowers. Grand enough for The Royal Enclosure, at their simplest they are still ideal for a country wedding.

Two of the most memorable flower-inspired designs: Tiffany lamps and Crown Derby china frame a simple arrangement of English country flowers

The English style of flower arranging

Over the years the English have developed a characteristic style of flower arrangement which is completely different from the way people in other parts of the world use them. The English style uses large quantities of flowers. The effect is as if you had wandered round your flower garden picking everything you fancied, and dropped the resulting armful of blooms straight into the nearest vase. The technical term for this tyle is massed flowers. You can see examples raised up on pedestals in churches, and people fill their fireplaces with

A typically Tudor use of flowers: garlands around the fireplace and fragrant blooms and boughs in the hearth. The floor itself is strewn with sweet-scented rushes

them in summer. It is a very adaptable idea, though not quite as uncontrived as it looks. To find out how such a characteristic style evolved, we must go back to medieval times.

In those days, ordinary people would have spent most of their time just trying to subsist. Gardens were useful rather than ornamental, mostly for growing vegetables and herbs. Monks grew quantities of herbs for their medicinal properties. There was no handy Boots branch on the corner in those days, and if you wanted medicine or cosmetics the chances were you would have to concoct them yourself. The nobility had a few home comforts in the shape of rushes scattered on the floors as the forerunner to modern carpets, mingled with herbs to kill the smells of an insanitary society. They used branches in fireplaces during the summer, but one of the few forms of household decoration was garlands of greenery, sometimes with flowers, hung round the walls. The idea of using garlands may well have been spontaneous, but since the theme occurs in classical architecture it seems likely that it may have been a Roman import.

However it started, the use of garlands lasted a long time because they were still much in evidence in Elizabethan times. By then, more flowers were being grown, and garlands consequently became more colourful. Owners of large houses often had knot gardens, where neatly clipped box hedges surrounded very formal beds filled with flowers. Hedges were grown alongside and over pathways to make covered arches,

A Georgian-style
flower arrangement
set in a classical urn of
the same period.
*Arranged by Pamela
South*

and evergreens were trimmed into fancy shapes, starting a
new fashion for topiary. But because there had been little
overseas exploration there was still a limited selection of plants
and flowers compared with today.

The gillyflower, a kind of carnation with clove-scented
flowers brought over by the Normans, was used not only in
garlands, but to make mulled wine – hence its popular name of
sops-in-wine. For the same reason, it was commonly found
growing outside public houses. Some kinds of roses,
honeysuckles, violets, marigolds, irises and primroses existed.
In fact some of the flowers popular then are relatively
uncommon now – Jack-in-hose primroses, for instance, which
have a green 'skirt' surrounding the petals. Flowers were
arranged in cooking or drinking utensils, not in purpose-made
vases as we know them now.

As history progressed, new kinds of flowers were gradually
introduced from abroad. The rich came to have bigger and
more comfortable houses, and more time to devote to the finer
things in life, which would have included having formal
gardens laid out, and entertaining fashionable friends in well-
furnished and attractively decorated rooms.

Over the centuries, the arrangement of flowers became
more organized, using vases of different kinds. The style of
country house gardens changed in the eighteenth century to
the 'natural' landscapes of Capability Brown. Since formal
flower beds played no part in his avenues of trees and vistas

opening onto ruined temples and ornamental lakes, flowers were relegated to the vegetable garden.

Whilst all these changes exerted a great effect on the lives and surroundings of people, living in the grand country houses, ordinary folk managed with what has become accepted as the English cottage garden. Here, vegetables, herbs and flowers would all have been grown together.

By the time the Victorians appeared on the scene, society contained a relatively affluent middle class. The rich were richer than ever, and the middle classes were out to copy them. As fast as the rich took to something new, the middle classes developed their cheaper versions. Unless you could keep up in the status stakes, you were nobody.

Top amongst the fashionable status symbols were flowers. The super-rich had enormous conservatories and hothouses in which their gardeners grew exotic flowers. The famous conservatory at Chatsworth, designed by Joseph Paxton, was so huge that when Queen Victoria and Prince Albert visited, their carriage drove right inside it. Such vast expanses of glass required a great deal of labour not only to look after, but to fill in the first place. There were teams of gardeners and squads of sponsored plant hunters whose job it was to be certain that their employers were the first to have the latest imports. New plants were pouring into the country from all over the world, but being a plant collector in those days was not glamorous. Relatively few of them lived to see how their discoveries fared back home – a good many collectors perished at the hands of hostile tribes, or succumbed to wild animals and tropical diseases.

Enormous fortunes were made out of orchids, and even plants such as coleus, common today but then a most exotic tropical rarity. Garden design reverted to the ultra-formal, and gardeners' lads were taught geometry to help them lay out elaborate bedding schemes with mathematical precision. Since head gardeners did not want their prize beds ruined by cutting, special flower beds for cutting were laid out elsewhere in the garden.

Trying their hardest to keep up with their betters were the middle classes. Lacking the wide open spaces of the country house owners, they did the best they could with scaled-down conservatories packed with plants and with their parlours. Aspidistras, Boston ferns, clivias and most of all palms were the pot plants they all had to have. Wardian cases, looking like miniature conservatories, were to be found in most fashionable parlours. These were domesticated versions of the collapsible plant cases used by plant hunters to transport their new discoveries safely back to England. The original cases were simple affairs into which plants were sealed to protect them on the long sea voyages home by creating a miniature version of the conditions in which they normally thrived. The domestic versions were chiefly used for plants such as orchids and ferns, where they acted in much the same way as a greenhouse, protecting the tender inmates from draughts and sudden changes of temperature as well as maintaining the necessary high humidity round them.

One of the most fascinating uses to which flowers were put was in making love letters. Victorian morality dictated that well brought up young men and women had few opportunities for getting to know one another unless they were actually engaged. Young ladies were very heavily chaperoned if a man was present. Young people solved the problem by sending messages in the 'language of flowers' – secret love letters disguised as posies. The idea was not invented by the Victorians. It originated in the east, in Moslem lands, and was brought back to this country by an English lady who wrote a dictionary of the symbolism of flowers. The idea caught on, and eventually there were so many flower dictionaries that different meanings were attributed to the same flowers. The serious suitor must have had terrible problems caused by misunderstandings unless he and his lady-love both owned the same version. The whole thing was further complicated by the fact that different species of the same flower sometimes had widely different meanings. A simple error caused by a mistaken plant name could completely alter the message – for instance from good wishes (sweet basil) to hatred (ordinary basil) – totally ruining an otherwise carefully conducted courtship. Some very odd posies must also have been presented with mushrooms, cacti and Venus fly traps all making up part of a message.

Fortunately the Victorian lady had little to occupy her time, so reading her flowers would have come as light relief from the activities of piano playing, watercolour painting and making pressed flower pictures which normally filled her day. And high among the most important of a young lady's accomplishments was arranging flowers.

One book for young ladies describes how to make a floral pavement, cautiously advising that it should be made somewhere it would not get walked on. The idea was based on Italian mosaic floors, but in this case the pattern was marked out on the floor with sand, and was filled in with thick layers of flower petals. For a longer-lasting pavement, damp sand or moss was spread on the floor and flower heads were pushed into it. Another flower manual describes how to decorate a ballroom with a wall of flowers, and then create an artificial rockery out of blocks of ice with creeping plants between them. One such rockery, at a ball given by the Prince and Princess of Wales for the Tsarina of Russia, used ten tons of ice in this way. For more simple occasions such as garden parties, details are given for building a rose arbour – not the sort of rustic building with roses growing over it that you might imagine, but a combination of trellis and marquee, covered with hundreds or thousands of fresh rose heads. A scaled down version of the

A Victorian posy in a silver container – a lady would have carried it while dancing, and then extended the legs so as to be able to sit it beside her plate at dinner

rustic outdoor rose arbour might be recreated indoors for special occasions, again using cut flowers.

One of the biggest leaps forward in flower arranging was the arrival of the table centre. Until the mid-nineteenth century, flowers had not really figured as dinner table decorations. True to form, the Victorians went completely overboard with them. Hostesses outdid one another in trying to come up with more and more flamboyant table centres. Fashions changed almost from week to week, so much so that books and magazines with articles on how to do them could scarcely keep pace.

The epergne was probably the best-known Victorian table centre. Built like a multi-storey vase, an epergne housed huge, tiered arrangements. Some apparently got so out of hand that after-dinner speakers had difficulty making themselves seen through the horticultural abundance in front of them. Flowers would also be placed above the table, hanging in conch shells or chandelier arrangements. They would be made into arches soaring over the table, with streamers of flowers trailing to each place setting from a table centre arrangement. Each guest might have his own private arrangement alongside his plate. Or maybe there would be a palm tree surrounded by flowers apparently sprouting through the table top itself. Indeed, some actually did – it was not unknown for a fashion-conscious hostess to cut a spare leaf of her table in half, and carve out a niche for the palm trees to 'grow' through.

But a reaction was inevitable. Towards the end of the Victorian era there was already the beginning of a move back to a more natural use of flowers and plants. Mrs Beeton refers somewhat scathingly to the overdone table centres of the Victorians. She felt that flowers were most effective if they were simple, and went on to give as an example a table for six to twelve guests on which the decorations would consist of up to four bowls of flowers, four candlesticks, and six dishes of almonds and preserved fruit. All this sounds anything but simple to us today. But despite the simplicity of her 'everyday' dinner parties, she nevertheless felt it was permissible to let rip a bit for a special occasion. At a dinner for a Very Important Airman she laid the table out like an airfield, complete with model aeroplanes suspended over the table by strings.

Being best known for her cookery, Mrs Beeton did make up for her 'simple' floral decorations by using edible flowers, both real and artificial, to decorate the food itself. Cutlets were frequently served covered in a sauce which made the perfect background to flowers made from sliced olives and other goodies. To prevent guests becoming entirely overpowered – Mrs Beeton was of course best known for recipes along the lines of 'take a quart of cream and two dozen eggs' – she also cautions of the perils of too heavily scented flowers in a warm room. Gardenias, stephanotis and hyacinths, all popular table centre flowers, were to be used sparingly.

Not until Constance Spry did the familiar triangular arrangement of what we now accept as the English style come into being. She was a florist who pioneered something completely different for the social events of her day, and then went on to found a flower arranging school for professional florists. Her students were taught how to do the most detailed work, and were sent off to make the famous Constance Spry-style arrangements at all kinds of functions.

Thus, the English way with flowers has changed greatly over the years. It continues to change, keeping up with a changing society and with new lifestyles.

Making a start

If you are new to flower arranging, ignore the old wives' tales – you do not need a special talent for it, nor do you need to be artistically inclined. You do not have to remember dozens of rules and regulations. The secret of making an arrangement that looks like one, instead of just a handful of flowers in a vase, is to know a few very basic tips. A good many teachers of flower arranging have their own magic formulae for making an arrangement. Follow these, and you will be surprised at what you can achieve. And although it is a good idea to start with something simple, the same formula can be used to make any kind of English-style arrangement, from the smallest miniature, to the largest pedestal and fireplace arrangement.

The technicalities

LOOKING AFTER CUT FLOWERS

There is more to flower arranging than just making them look attractive. If you are going to spend time arranging them you might as well take a few minutes longer to make sure that they will last well too. This is what flower arrangers call 'conditioning'.

The reason you need to do it is that as soon as a flower is cut, the column of sap in its stem is broken; since the flower is still drawing sap upwards, the cells at the bottom of the stem soon become filled with air. The longer the flower is out of water, the longer the column of air in the stem becomes. Merely putting the flower in water is not enough because, although water is once again coming in at the bottom of the stem, there is now a bubble of air moving towards the top. If you can prevent the flower stem from bunging itself up with air and keep it full of water instead, then your flowers will last very much longer.

At its simplest, conditioning involves cutting the bottom inch or two off the stems of the flowers when you get them home. Do this under water, and you'll be certain that no air can find its way inside the stem. Some flowers have special requirements for conditioning – those that produce lots of sap, like poppies, need to have the cut ends of their stems sealed to keep the sap in. This is done by singeing them in a flame. Plants with hollow stems, such as angelica, need to be held upside down, filled with water and plugged. Flowers with very long stems that are a little tired after a long journey, or which have started to wilt, are best rejuvenated by soaking them completely rather than just putting the ends in water. If you have a deep bucket, stand them in tepid water up to the necks. Otherwise you can lay them out flat in the bath; again, water with the chill taken off is best, especially in cold weather.

Most of the flowers you buy from a florist will already have been very thoroughly conditioned before you buy them; but because they will be taken out of water again for the trip home, it is still advisable to recut the stems under water when you get them home. If you cut flowers from the garden, put them straight into water if you possibly can.

Even after you have arranged flowers, water in the stems can still cause problems. Unless you change the water regularly, bacteria will breed in it and make the water go green, slimy and smelly. The bacteria will also block up the flowers' water-transporting cells, so that they wilt even though they are not short of water.

People have tried adding all sorts of peculiar things to the water to make flowers last longer. Some people swear by aspirins, others by sugar or fizzy lemonade, and yet others even give their flowers the pill. The Victorians always used to think that putting a few geranium leaves in an arrangement would make flowers last.

More scientifically, horticultural research stations have looked at the problem, and so far results indicate that fizzy lemonade is probably just as good as commercial flower life additives. But even without using any special products you can make flowers last longer simply by using clean vases and clean water, and by making sure the stems are full of water in the first place.

KEEPING FLOWERS IN THEIR PLACE

One of the hardest things about arranging flowers, unless you are already in the know, is making them stay where you want them. Basically there are three ways of holding flowers in position: scrunched up chicken wire, pinholders and floral foam. To avoid disaster, the thing that holds your flowers in place needs holding in place itself. You can stick pinholders down with plasticine-like material; chicken wire and foam may wedge in place inside a narrow vase – otherwise you can get gadgets like suction pads on sticks to hold them in place.

Each kind of flower-holding gadget is best for a specific purpose, and no amount of struggling will make it do for the wrong kinds of flower. Scrunched up chicken wire is best for woody-stemmed material, such as branches and heavy chrysanthemums. Pinholders only work well with material that has fairly thick, fleshy stems – the pins are pushed into the bottom of the stems; jamming them between the pins does not work. Floral foam is best used for flowers with reasonably thin, wiry stems; soft, thick stems do not push into it properly. It comes in blocks that have to be cut to fit different-shaped vases, and this is most easily done with a sharp knife while the stuff is dry. It then needs to be soaked in water for ten or fifteen minutes before it is ready to use. There are two kinds of floral foam: the green is for fresh flowers and the brown for dried. Long before floral foam was invented, people used to arrange flowers in vases full of damp sand. The Victorians went one better, growing their own live floral foam. They rooted cuttings of club moss in containers of damp sand, and pushed the flowers in among the frothy foliage. You can still do so today if you run out of the modern version.

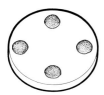

The base of a pinholder.
Stick 4 blobs of plasticene or flower arranger's fixative to the underside.

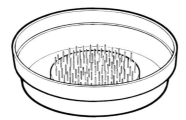

Stick the pinholder firmly down in the centre of a 4½-inch plastic plant pot saucer. (Both the saucer and the base of the pinholder must be dry or they won't stick)

Next, cut a piece of floral foam (commonly known as oasis) to the required shape – here a circle – and soak it in a bowl of water for 2 minutes; then push it firmly onto the pins of the pinholder. (Oasis also comes in oblong blocks, which can easily be cut to shape with a sharp knife to fit odd-shaped containers). This gives a firm foundation into which to fit your flowers

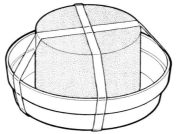

If using heavy flowers, you can stretch sticky tape over the oasis to hold it down – a sort of belt-and-braces job. A special tape is available from flower arrangers' supply shops, but Sellotape will do

Making a traditional English flower arrangement*

The following step-by-step explanations and drawings are put forward as a guide only. Flower arranging is a very personal thing, and you can adapt to your own taste, develop your own design.

Start with five flowers of the same colour and variety but not necessarily the same size. In fact, try to get different sizes – easily done with flowers from your garden, not so easy with a bunch from the florist. Condition them in a bucket or the bath, and cut the stems to different lengths. Try to make the stems look as though they are coming from one central point somewhere in the middle of your block of foam: flower No. 1 is straight and upright, No. 2 leans slightly back. Nos. 3 and 4 are angled forward and No. 5 comes forward over the edge of your dish. (See drawing opposite).

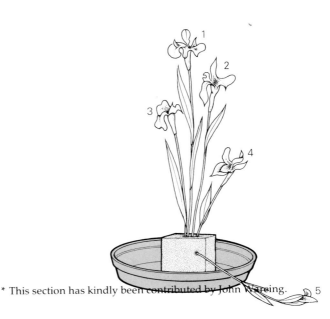

* This section has kindly been contributed by John Wareing.

Now add some leaves
and branches, which
have also been
conditioned in a
bucket or the bath.
Choose leaves in scale
with the flowers you
are using, and try to
add variety in shapes
and colours. Disguise
your foam with one or
two larger leaves
which have been cut
shorter on the stem.

Now add a further five
flowers. Choose them
to blend in colour with
the first five, and keep
them in scale. Nos. 6
and 7 face to the back
of the design, No. 8 is
cut very short to the
middle and Nos. 9 and
10 come forward over
the front of your
container.

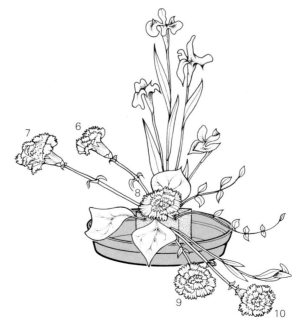

Finally add five more flowers: No. 11 facing to the rear, No. 12 upright, and 13, 14 and 15 angled towards you. Add one or two more leaves and you have a traditional English design.

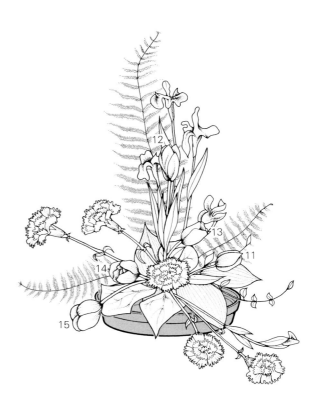

Although you have placed the three types of flowers in irregular lines in different directions in your arrangement, the finished effect looks like a mass of different colours. Now, you can of course go on adding more flowers or the same varieties or introduce other colours.

The flower stems need not be more than 1½ inches into the foam, to be secure.

After finishing the arrangement, look around your house for a shallow dish – even something as simple as one from the kitchen may well fit the bill. Place the plant pot saucer in the dish, fill it with water and check the level each day; top up as necessary.

One final word: enjoy your arranging, put the flowers in as you want to do. If you are happy with them that is all that matters.

If you want to look for further instruction, the majority of local authorities have evening classes for flower arranging. I would urge you to find the venue where your local flower arranging club meets.

Flower clubs, shows and exhibitions

The flower show is a typically English institution. It started towards the end of the Victorian era when corners were set aside for classes of arranged flowers at horticultural shows. The first-ever class – for an arrangement in an epergne – was won by a man, and though women have tended to dominate the arena since, the few men who do participate tend to be very successful.

Nowadays, far from being only a corner at horticultural shows, there are now some 1,250 flower arrangement clubs with close to 100,000 members all over the UK. The governing body of all these clubs is NAFAS, the National Association of Flower Arrangement Societies, which has recently celebrated its silver jubilee.

The aim of NAFAS is to coordinate the activities of flower clubs all over the country; it undertakes the training and qualifying of flower arranging instructors and judges as well as organizing competitions and exhibitions at national level. NAFAS also produces some excellent, low-priced information sheets on various aspects of flower arranging, which are the ideal starting place for beginners.

Members of NAFAS keep in touch with what is going on in the flower arranging world via their own quarterly magazine, *The Flower Arranger*, which contains articles for beginners and experts alike. If you want to join a flower club, and do not know where your nearest one is, NAFAS will put you in touch – their address is in the information section at the end of this book.

A flower club is the ideal place to learn flower arranging. These clubs invite visiting demonstrators and lecturers on topics of interest, such as plants for flower arrangers. Very often clubs will have a sales table where you can buy special equipment, which can often be difficult to find elsewhere. Besides teaching flower arranging, clubs normally run their own shows and help newcomers who are interested in moving up the rungs of the competition ladder. For those not interested in competitive flower arranging, it is still very interesting to visit shows, as other people's arrangements can often provide new ideas. Shows are also the place to see a wide variety of styles of flower arranging. Shows at small clubs are friendly affairs where you can have a go just for fun, and to see how your flower arranging is coming on.

Not all the classes at shows are the 'Arrangement of Spring Flowers in a Bowl' kind. A good many, especially at bigger shows, call for the arranger to interpret the title of the class – which may be a film title, the name of a book or something similar. The kind of things the judge will be looking for are how well the arranger has designed the exhibit, the suitability of the container, whether the flowers are well cared for, and how well the class theme has been interpreted. If you visit a few large shows, you will soon be able to see from the prizewinning exhibits how experienced competitors go about it. A vivid imagination undoubtedly helps in competition work, as does remembering to read the small print. One of the most important things a competition arrangement must do is abide by the rules of its class – any that do not are automatically disqualified, which is a great waste of time and effort. Successful exhibitors tend to upgrade themselves from smaller shows to larger ones until they reach national or even international level, and once they reach the very top, some decide to opt out of the race altogether and turn to exhibition work instead.

The main difference between exhibitions and competitions is that participants in exhibitions are not restricted by the rules of a particular class. They have the freedom to 'do their own thing'. Frequently, top-class exhibitors are invited to participate in special events such as festivals at stately homes, cathedrals and other rather grand locations. There are also less high-powered exhibitions which give people who do not happen to like competing the opportunity to have a free hand to try out their ideas in a different environment.

If you want to see both competition and exhibition work in one place, there is one show that is an absolute necessity. Unlike many which are one-off events, this takes place regularly, every year: it is the Chelsea Flower Show. Every year, more people than ever before cram themselves into the Royal Hospital grounds to see magnificent displays of flowers and plants. Chelsea stands out from all the other shows because here you can see a whole year's flowers in bloom at the same time. This feat is all the more impressive because, unlike most flower shows, which take place in the summer when flowers are easy to come by, Chelsea takes place in May during that awkward gap after the spring flowers but long before most of the summer flowers. Yet there they all are, flowering together just for that one special week – roses, delphiniums and begonias rubbing shoulders with spring bulbs. Many of them will have been specially treated to advance or retard their natural flowering season.

Several countries use Chelsea as a shop window for their produce. Venezuela, the Netherlands and South Africa provide lavish exhibits of cut flowers. Our own National Farmers' Union does the same sort of thing in vegetables. All the flower organizations are here too – Interflora on the floristry side, and NAFAS representing the flower arrangers.

Outside the main marquee there are people selling flower paintings or flower arranging accessories, and even giving flowers away. But the real highlight of Chelsea from the flower arranger's point of view has an area all to itself – the flower arrangers' marquee. It is always packed with visitors, and usually there is a long queue. If you want a chance to wander

The National Farmers' Union Market Produce Society stand in the main marquee at the Chelsea Flower Show

round in peace and quiet you must get there early in the morning, soon after the show opens at 8 am. And if that seems like an early start, spare a thought for the poor exhibitors, many of whom will have been up for most of the night before the show opened, putting the finishing touches to their creations.

Impressive though a show like Chelsea certainly is, the work that goes on behind the scenes to get it all together is even more so. Hundreds of tons of fragile materials have to be transported there, usually at the last minute to make sure that everything is as fresh as it possibly can be. For lots of nurserymen exhibitors, showing at Chelsea means leaving the rest of the business to look after itself, so they cannot be away for very long. Once at the show, there's a stand to be built, electricity to be laid on, and plants and flowers to be cared for and arranged. Many exhibitors practically move in with their charges during those last few days before the show. Large exhibitors such as the South Africans use one team of contractors to build their stands for them, and another – professional florists this time – to arrange their produce for them. Sometimes they need to be acrobats as much as flower arrangers, since some of their exhibits involve arrangements perched at the tips of branches on a tree.

The NAFAS display, on the other hand, is entirely designed and manned by members. Top amateur arrangers working in teams build up the design that has taken many months to plan in fine detail. In the flower arrangers' marquee, participants in the individual competition are hard at work on their entries. This is not the first time that most of them will have made up their particular arrangement; they will have had several practice sessions at home before the event, while they were still formulating their ideas.

Again, Chelsea is unlike other flower shows, because it has classes for the professional florist as well as for the amateur arranger. Normally the public are unlikely to see professionals competing against each other – they usually do so only at their own competitions to which the public are not admitted. It is interesting to have the opportunity to see how professional and amateur shape up to each other. The biggest difference between the two groups shows behind the scenes. The amateurs take the greatest time and trouble over their work, whereas the professionals, used to working to a daily deadline, are in and out and back to their hotels for drinks before dinner, leaving their amateur colleagues still hard at it. This is the place to see the midnight oil burning, and opening night nerves.

When is a vase not a vase?

Not everything that looks like a vase was originally meant for putting flowers in. Over the ages many vases have been made that were never intended to take flowers, while lots of flowers have been put into things that were not vases. So how can one tell which were flower vases and which were other kinds of vases? Even the experts cannot always say. But the strange thing is that, despite all the vases in museums and collections, containers have never played an important part in the English style of flower arranging. Generally anything that held water was acceptable – it was the flowers that mattered most. As time progressed, the standard of drinking receptacles rose. By Tudor times people were drinking out of pewter, so it seems likely that they would have put flowers in pewter tankards. Later, glass and silver containers were brought into use.

A typical Chelsea
Flower Show exhibit,
South Down
Nursery's display
includes both cut
flowers and plants

It was probably not until about the seventeenth century that things became more formal, and a good many vases started to come into the country from abroad. Chinese vases were the fashionable things to have, and to cater for the growing demand a Dutch pottery factory started making copies of the Chinese designs, keeping to the blue and white patterns that have now become familiar as Delft. One of their most successful lines was sets of five matching Chinese-looking vases for the mantelpiece, usually with two upright jars which could have been used for flowers, and three smaller pots with lids. Another popular style was the 'brick', a rectangular vase with a lid pierced with holes through which flowers were pushed. One of the best known of the Delft designs does not seem to have been copied from the Chinese – their tulip vases bore more than a passing resemblance to the many-spouted vases found in ancient Egyptian tombs.

British china factories such as Derby and Worcester made dinner services for the rich and titled, but they also made vases. Some were meant not for flowers but for potpourri – the Victoria and Albert Museum has a particularly ornate example of a Chelsea potpourri vase shaped like a dovecote complete with doves flying in and out. Other factories sold their vases already arranged with porcelain flowers.

The classical style came in for a big revival towards the end of the eighteenth century, and for a while the Grecian urn look was fashionable. In fact the original Grecian urns were not used for flowers, but would have held oil or wine. In France, the Sèvres factory was making vases for the elegant salons of the day. Fashionable ladies entertained in their boudoirs and needed suitably elaborate vases, both for use and as ornaments.

By high Victorian times, all semblance of taste had gone and bric-à-brac was in vogue. Potted plants stood in jardinières or ornamental pot covers, and in the same way that chairs had antimacassars, no vase was complete without its own little mat. Epergnes stood in the middle of tables, pairs of decorated glass vases on mantelpieces, bowls on occasional tables and pianos, and purely decorative vases of all sorts – silver, porcelain or glass – anywhere else that there was room. The well brought up Victorian young lady also made her own vases. The art of potichomanie was a nice, respectable, time-consuming hobby. Here, pictures were stuck onto the inside of a plain glass vase. Birds and flowers were favourite subjects. The inside of the glass was then painted; when it was dry, the pictures were waterproofed with a coat of varnish. The result was intended to look like high-class porcelain.

The arrival of art nouveau around 1900 brought in what must have seemed at the time very unusual vases. Major technological advances had been achieved in glassmaking, so many of the art nouveau vases involved some extraordinary effects. Plant designs were much used, and not only as patterns; they would often form part of the structure.

So what really determined whether a vase was to be used for flowers? The same criterion must have held true in historical times as does now – price. Anything very precious, hand-made or rare would most likely have been too valuable to risk damaging by using it for flowers. Even nowadays, when we take relatively inexpensive, mass-produced items for granted, there are craftsmen still making by hand vases which could be the collectors' pieces of the future. Would you risk putting flowers in tomorrow's antiques?

Growing flowers for English-style arranging

The English way of arranging flowers resembles our particular style of gardening. Traditionally, both make use of masses of flowers, in the biggest colour range possible, and all packed closely together. Herbaceous border flowers (perennials) are the mainstay of both garden planting and flower arrangements, with annual flowers and shrubs such as roses filling out the spaces in between. But, since both gardening and flower arranging have come a long way during the course of their respective histories, things have changed; newly introduced plants have given us a wider than ever range of plant material to choose from, and new ways of growing traditional favourites now make much lighter work of gardening. This is just as well, since few of us can afford to keep the armies of gardeners who once tended the traditional herbaceous borders.

So let's look in more detail at how to lay out a modern garden with flower arranging in mind, and consider some specially useful plants well worth finding room for.

EASY GARDENING, ENGLISH STYLE

Traditional versus mixed borders

The traditional English garden consisted of separate shrubbery, herbaceous border and formal beds filled with annual flowers, often with separate beds of flowers for cutting. But now that gardens are smaller, and people often have less time to spend to look after them, we tend to prefer mixed borders, where shrubs, flowers and bulbs grow together. This way it is easy to ensure that the whole garden looks colourful and interesting all year round: we can choose a selection of spring-flowering bulbs, summer-flowering annuals and herbaceous plants, and shrubs for autumn colour, winter bark, and flowers and catkins in spring. It is not difficult to include among them a good selection for cutting to bring indoors.

The following plants are all easy to grow in mixed borders, and provide useful material for flower arranging, English style.

Alstroemeria	Herbaceous
Artichoke	Herbaceous
Aster, especially var. Ostrich Plume	Half-hardy annual
Calendula (English marigold)	Hardy annual
Camellia	Shrub
Carnation, border	Herbaceous
Chrysanthemum, garden-flowering	Frost-tender perennial
Chrysanthemum, Korean	Herbaceous

Cornflower	Hardy annual
Dahlia	Frost-tender perennial; some varieties, such as Coltness, can be grown from seed like half-hardy annuals
Delphinium	Herbaceous
Freesia	Bulbs planted in autumn – be sure to choose varieties suitable for outdoor growing, rather than greenhouse kinds which are not easy
Garrya elliptica	Evergreen shrub with long, greenish catkins in spring
Gladiolus	Bulb
Gypsophila	Hardy annual; lots of tiny flowers, usually white, looking like foam
Hosta	Herbaceous plant grown for ornamental glaucous green or variegated foliage
Liatris	Herbaceous
Lily	Bulb
Paeony	Herbaceous
Pansy	Hardy perennial
Pink	Herbaceous
Rose	Shrub
Rudbeckia	Half-hardy annual
Schizanthus	(Poor man's orchid) Half-hardy annual for greenhouse border or outdoor bedding
Sweet pea	Hardy annual
Sweet william	Hardy annual if sown early, otherwise hardy biennial
Viola	Hardy perennial
Zinnia	Half-hardy annual

Unusual 'cutting' flowers to try

Antirrhinum	Half-hardy annual
Cyclamen	Greenhouse or house plant; if you have a greenhouse grow your own from seed, and use the spares for flowers for cutting. Plants take sixteen months to flower from seed
Eucomis (pineapple flower)	Unusual plant grown from bulbs; not frost-hardy so best grown in pots and brought into the greenhouse in winter. Can be grown from seed but takes several years

	to flower. Flowers last eight weeks in water
Geranium (pelargonium, or zonal geranium)	Frost-tender perennial that can be grown outdoors in summer, but needs to be kept in a heated greenhouse or indoors in winter
Sweet Basil var. Dark Opal	Half-hardy annual; a culinary herb with unusual dark red-black leaves that make a useful foil to red and orange flowers

Borders versus island beds

The traditional border was just that – a bed that bordered the edge of the garden, usually with a hedge running along the back of it. And they were a lot of work to look after for several reasons, most of which involved the hedge. Hedge bottoms are notorious for harbouring pests which creep out and attack the plants; weeds, too, spread from them out into the border, making lots of work. And the shade of the hedge made the plants grow tall, lanky and weak, so herbaceous ones in particular had to be staked to keep them upright. Today, island beds are much more popular, and blend in much better with modern houses and small gardens; a bed is cut out of the lawn, usually in an informal shape such as a teardrop. Because you have all-round access to it, an island bed is easy to weed without treading on the soil. And because the plants are not growing in the shade, they are sturdier and less likely to need staking. In any case, modern varieties of herbaceous plants are generally bred to be shorter, so staking is becoming a thing of the past.

Weedkillers

This is another way of making life easy for yourself in the garden. Although the weedkiller section of your local garden centre can look rather daunting, staff will usually be happy to advise on what is suitable for which purpose. Total weedkillers kill absolutely everything: Tumbleweed, sold by Murphy's, is useful for clearing weeds from a new piece of ground before you plant it – once the weeds are dead, a few weeks after use, the ground can safely be planted. Path weedkillers not only kill everything, but generally stop anything else from growing for the rest of the season too, so are most economically used in spring. They are intended for use on paths, drives and patios, but not between plants.

Other kinds of weedkillers are selective. Caseron G can be applied between established trees and shrubs, but not among flowers. It is best used in spring, and since it does not actually kill existing weeds it should be put down just after hoeing, to keep the ground free of weeds for the rest of the season.

Covershield can be used between flowers as well as among trees and shrubs, but only lasts ten weeks or so before you need to make another application. Even so, two to three doses a year should be sufficient to obviate weeding; again, this product does not kill existing weeds, so you must use it after hoeing when it will stop new weeds coming up. Strong-growing perennial weeds such as couch grass, thistles and nettles may still come through, but can easily be dealt with by a squirt from an aerosol path weedkiller such as Fison's. Make sure it does not touch any plants you want to keep, though.

HOW TO GROW . . .

Hardy annuals (HA)

These are raised each year from seed, but are about the easiest of plants to grow as you simply sow them where you want them to flower in spring. This can be done from February onwards, providing the weather is not too cold or the ground saturated with water. Prepare the soil first by forking and raking, adding peat or compost if the soil is poor, and a handful of general fertilizer such as Growmore per square yard of bed. Then scatter the seed very thinly, and rake lightly over the area to cover it with soil. To get the best effect, instead of sowing in straight rows scatter the seed over an irregularly shaped area to produce an informal group of plants. Even better, grow several different kinds of hardy annuals together in groups, keeping the taller varieties to the back. Mark out the bed first with the point of a cane, and scatter each variety separately in its own patch. After sowing, you need only water if the weather is very dry; to keep flowers blooming longer remove the dead heads regularly.

Half-hardy annuals (HHA)

These are the group of plants we normally think of as bedding plants. Because frost kills them they cannot be planted outside until around the end of May. To sow seed outside so late would mean that the plants were only just coming into flower in autumn, which would rather defeat the object of the exercise. To have plants in flower for late May you need to sow the seed in early March in a heated greenhouse, preferably inside a heated propagator to provide a sufficiently high temperature (60–70°F) to start with. Once the seeds are up and the seedlings big enough to handle, you can 'prick them out' – transplant them – in seed trays; allow each seedling about a square inch of space. At this stage the seedlings do not need quite so much heat, but they still do best if you can keep the temperature above 50°F, though it can go down to 40°F at times without too much harm. People sometimes manage to raise bedding plant seedlings on a window sill indoors, and while the temperature there may be higher than in a greenhouse, there is often not enough light and the seedlings become long and spindly; as a result, they often die from a fungal infection as they are too weak to resist it. If you do not have the right conditions for growing bedding plants yourself from seed, it is better to buy them from a garden centre. Again, removing dead flower heads from plants will prolong flowering.

Herbaceous plants

These are more expensive to buy than annuals, but at least because they are perennial you don't have to keep replacing them. For this reason, growing them involves less work. The best time to buy plants is in spring or autumn; put them into the ground straightaway. Container-grown plants can be planted all through the summer, even when they are in flower, but you will then need to water them regularly.

In autumn, when the foliage dies off, cut herbaceous plants down to just above ground level and burn the dead leaves and stems. When the clumps get too big, every few years, dig them up, split them into pieces and replant them, thus increasing your stock of plants. This is best done in autumn or spring.

Frost-tender perennials

This group covers some of the most attractive garden flowers, such as dahlias, chrysanthemums and geraniums. The plants cannot be left out in the garden in winter since they would be killed by frost, so they are dug up and kept in a frost-free place until spring. Dahlias die back in autumn to leave just their tubers, which can be stored in a shed; they must be perfectly dry or they risk rotting, and must be kept away from mice. Cut back chrysanthemums in autumn, and dig up the 'stool' or crown. The stools must be kept in a heated greenhouse or porch, and in spring you can use the young shoots as cuttings. Plant out the rooted cuttings, and the throw away the old roots. Old geranium plants can be replanted, but it is better to use them for cuttings, too, as new plants flower better than old. For really early flowering plants it is better to take cuttings in late summer, and root them on a window sill or in a frost-free greenhouse. Alternatively, grow them from seed sown in very early spring.

Bulbs

Most garden bulbs are spring-flowering and are therefore sold in the late summer and autumn. Plant them soon after you buy them, certainly not later than November. Lily bulbs tend to be sold in spring and should be planted then.

Bulb flowers are seen to best advantage planted informally in groups, naturalized among trees and shrubs; narcissi and other low-growing spring bulbs can also be naturalized in grass, or on banks, but not in deep shade. Once planted, there is no need to move them unless they proliferate freely and become too dense, when flowering may suffer. If you have planted bulbs in grass, avoid mowing that area or using a lawn weedkiller until after the flowers and foliage have died down naturally.

Shrubs and roses

Traditionally, shrubs and roses were always sold and planted in autumn or spring, because they could only be moved while the roots were dormant. But now that plants are grown in containers they can be transplanted at any time of year, though if you plant in summer you must be prepared to water them regularly.

Hybrid tea roses must be pruned back to six inches above ground level each spring, around late March, otherwise they will not flower well. Other shrubs, including shrub roses, rarely need any pruning other than perhaps removing dead or rubbing branches or tidying up the shape, which is usually done immediately after flowering. Low, bushy, shrubby plants such as lavenders and heathers can be kept tidy by clipping them over with shears after flowering.

For best results feed shrubs and other plants in mixed borders in spring and early summer with one handful of general-purpose fertilizer such as Growmore per square yard of bed.

2 The Continental Style

What's so different?

Despite everything the politicians do to make us all into standard 'Europeans', you have only got to cross the Channel to see just how different things really are on the other side. It's not just the language that's different, but the scenery, the houses and the people, too. And, not surprisingly, they take a very different view from us of flowers and how to arrange them.

In Holland, for instance, people are crazy about indoor plants. All the houses are built with specially large windows to accommodate them. And as for curtains, they don't bother with them, other than a short, lacy frill round the top. Windows are quite definitely for plants. Even the barges working on the canals have pot plants in their windows. When there is no more room on the window sill itself, more space is created by dangling trailing plants from above. Rumour has it that some people actually build their window display purposely for the benefit of people looking in from the outside – it's nice to know that the businesslike Dutch are not immune from keeping up with the Joneses.

The range of plants you can buy in Holland is amazing – and they are not expensive. At such prices it's not difficult to understand why the Dutch are a nation of pot plant fanatics, because you can buy on a market stall plants for which a collector would give a small fortune back home. The more specialist plants are not, of course, so cheap as everyday ones. But in Holland they are not necessarily bought by collectors – anyone who takes a fancy to something unusual will have no trouble finding what they want.

Part of the reason for the indoor plant craze is that Holland is a small country where land is very expensive and most houses only have small gardens, or none at all. So to get the urge to grow out of their systems, most of the Dutch have to turn indoors. While the other northern Europeans are not quite so obsessed with pot plants as are the Dutch, they don't fall far behind. The further north you go, the worse the climate

Two views of the interior of a Dutch home. The photograph above
shows the effective use of massed plants in a sunny bay window; on
the right is an individual and most attractive display of plants

becomes for gardening outdoors, and the more do people have to indulge 'heir plant-growing needs indoors.

But social attitudes to plants on the Continent are different from in England. How many people do you know who continually cosset a sick or ancient plant, which has long since lost its leaves and its looks? In England, the gardening instinct is a strong one and we get much of our enjoyment out of actually looking after our plants – watering, feeding, repotting and taking cuttings. On the whole we like to buy smallish plants, so that we can have the fun of watching them grow. To the Continentals, it seems as if we make as much fuss of our plants as we do our pets, and they think it's just as odd. Their view of plants is completely different. A continental plant is there for one reason, and one reason only – it is part of the decor. In just the same way that you wouldn't expect to buy a footstool and watch it grow into a three-piece suite, the Dutch want a plant to be the right size when they buy it. Plants that are sick or old have no more place in the orderly Dutch interior

than a three-legged chair, or a carpet with a hole in it. Out they go with the rubbish, and in comes a new one, at the peak of perfection. As for growing your own plants – the idea is as ludicrous to them as trying to manufacture your own wallpaper. Very definitely it is a job best left to the professional. And the same holds true for their flowers.

From the number of high-class florists you pass in the high street of even the smallest of towns, you might easily be fooled into thinking that the Continentals are as keen on flower arranging as we are. But you would be wrong. True, they spend much more on flowers than we do; but most of them leave the arranging all to the florists. Instead of being a hobby, as they are over here, on the Continent flowers are one of life's social graces. Nobody would dream of going to a dinner party empty-handed – they would take flowers for the hostess, or maybe a box of chocolates. Husbands coming home from the office will pick up flowers at the railway station – most of the larger ones have a florist in the same way that British ones have a newspaper stall. Over here, most husbands would be embarrassed to be seen carrying a bunch of flowers; and most wives receiving them for no apparent reason immediately assume the worst of motives. The continental housewife, on the other hand, is much more likely to feel hard done by if she doesn't receive flowers quite often.

There are several ways of buying flowers from a continental florist that don't involve the recipient in any flower arranging. One way is to buy flowers already arranged in a vase or basket – all you need do is top up the water periodically. Florists keep a ready-made selection on the shelf. You can buy quite extraordinary arrangements – in Germany some include chicken wire, while others come in pre-formed cellophane posy holders. But it is a fashion-conscious business, and trends change fast.

Of course, you don't have to buy an off-the-peg arrangement. You might prefer to choose your own flowers from the florist's selection, and have them made into a 'hand bunch'. It takes only a couple of minutes. Right in front of your eyes. (The sequence of drawings on page 53 show you basic technique). The florist starts with the middle of the arrangement, holding the stems together in one hand and adding new flowers with the other. When it is finished, she ties the base of the stems tightly round with fine string, and gift wraps the whole thing for you. All you have to do when you get it home is remove the wrapping paper and put the bunch straight into a vase.

Apart from the ready-made arrangments, something else you would quickly notice anywhere on the Continent is that florists stock a lot of very strange and exotic blooms that you might easily not recognize. The reason is that, since they are such big buyers of flowers, the continentals are always on the look out for something different. Out-of-the-ordinary blooms

A continental 'hand bunch' in the process of being made (see explanatory drawings, page 53)

The same arrangement in its vase

rarely seen back home, such as gerberas, proteas, monkey paw, banksia, bird-of-paradise flower, orchids and anthurium all appear quite regularly in the average continental florist's shop.

In Holland, you can buy flowers in lots of other places besides florists. They sell them in kiosks at the side of the road, in many of their supermarkets, and in 'bucket shops' – open-fronted shops whose displays of flowers spill out all over the pavement so that people can hardly get by. The name comes from the buckets the flowers stand in; not that you could tell, all you can see is a solid carpet of flowers. In Amsterdam, you could pick up your flowers or plants at the famous floating flower market, so called because what look like market stalls from the front are actually perching on barges floating in the canal.

And if you need a bunch of flowers in a hurry after hours, there are always vending machines. Or were, I should say – as experiments go, this is one that failed. A few flower machines were introduced a few years back, but they didn't catch on as well as the inventors expected – it seems that the value-conscious Continentals don't trust flowers cooped up in a tin box all day, and prefer to buy what they can see in a shop.

WHERE DO THEY COME FROM?

Although most of the European countries grow some flowers of their own, Holland is especially famous. You might almost call it the greenhouse of Europe, because in Holland horticulture is a highly organized, major industry. In some parts of the country, as far as they eye can see there is nothing but greenhouses; acres and acres of them, growing just about every food crop you can think of – and of course flowers. It is a highly specialized business. Huge nurseries may have perhaps 10 acres of a single kind of flower growing in one enormous glasshouse employing the very latest in greenhouse technology.

Gerberas, large, brightly coloured daisy-like flowers originally from South Africa, grow in rows, each of which is heated by its own underground hot water pipe. The surrounding air is kept at a carefully controlled temperature, equivalent to that in a living room. And each plant has its very own piped food and water supply. To crown it all, they even get canned music played all day – though the people who look after them seem to appreciate it too. Picking gerberas is a complicated job. To make quite certain the flowers will last as long as they should in water, blooms are not cut the minute they open, as you might expect. Instead, you must wait until you can see two rings of stamens showing in the centre of the flower. Good eyesight is a 'must' if you want to be a Dutch flower picker. And when it comes to the latest fashion in gerberas, double-flowered varieties, you need intuition, because you just can't see the stamens among all those petals.

Packing such big, fragile flowers is a work of art in itself. The different grades are separated out from the buckets of blooms sent to the packing shed by the pickers. Each flower has its stem threaded through a backing board, and as soon as each board is full of flowers the stems are dunked in tepid water for a couple of hours so as to be fully charged by the time they are sent out. This individual attention pays dividends – without it the grower would not get top price for his flowers, and the customer would not get value for money. Properly handled from the outset, gerberas should last twelve to fourteen days in the vase – almost as long as they would on the plants.

Another 8-acre nursery specializes in orchids; but they don't sell the plants, just the cut flowers. These are made up into pre-packed buttonholes and sprays in presentation boxes, as well as being sold just as plain cut flowers. The plants grow in large pots, filled not with any sort of soil or compost, but with a synthetic growing medium. It looks very much like the floral foam used for arranging flowers, and, strange though it seems, the plants seem to thrive on it. Some growers use another synthetic medium, rockwool, which is more like the stuff used to insulate roofs, but although the plants like it, the people who work with them don't because sharp bits stick in their fingers. Once again, each plant has all mod cons laid on. But this grower does not spend his own time doing the sort of things a more traditional grower might. No one here opens ventilators, turns on taps for watering or mixes up fertilizer to make the plants' liquid feeds. It is all done by computer. If that goes wrong, as it did once when it was struck by lightning during a storm, pandemonium results.

Of the 10,000 acres of greenhouses in Holland, about half are used entirely for growing pot plants and cut flowers. That is an awful lot of flowers and plants to sell – and although the Dutch buy a large number themselves, very many more are sold all over Europe and even exported to more distant parts of the world.

To distribute so much highly perishable produce fast enough to stop it spoiling takes a lot of organization. To make sure that everything works efficiently, the Dutch have a network of produce auctions where buyers from anywhere in the world can come and buy. Flowers will be cut one day, sold at auction the following morning, and could be on sale in a florist's hundreds or even thousands of miles away the same evening.

A Dutch auction is not like a British one. Instead of starting at a low figure and raising it with each new bid, a Dutch auction works backwards, and you bid against a clock. The clock starts at a high figure, and as the hand rotates the price gradually goes down. Meanwhile the buyers sit watching intently, each in his own reserved seat in the auction room, with his own button to press when he wants to bid. Eventually somebody's nerve cracks and he presses his button. Then he has bought that particular lot – or as much of it as he wants. Each buyer has his own microphone through which he can tell the auctioneer how much of the lot he wants to buy if his bid is successful; then the clock starts off again, to sell what is left. During a few hours' trading, many millions of guilders' worth of produce changes hands.

The whole process is computerized from start to finish. As soon as flowers arrive at the auction from the growers they are loaded onto trucks and given a lot number. Then the truck is conveyed to the clock on a mechanically masterminded miniature railway. As each truck enters the auction hall, a scanner automatically reads the lot number, and the main computer relays onto the clock face all the information about the consignment. Buyers need the mental dexterity of a three-dimensional chess player to absorb all the detail before them *and* worry about making their bid. But they must get used to it all right, because the whole operation works very smoothly indeed.

After the auction, flowers for export can go straight to the airport. Other flowers, bought by small, independent wholesalers, will be loaded into vans and rushed to the nearest ferry or motorway, to be offered door-to-door on the regular round of florists. Flying Dutchmen, as the fleets of vans are called, visit any outlet that could possibly stock flowers – so long as it is no more than a day-trip away from the auction. But some flowers linger longer at the auction. Some larger wholesalers have their own work areas within the auction building, where relays of girls work to make up individual bunches of mixed flowers from the buckets of single colours

A 'Flying Dutchman' – an independent Dutch flower wholesaler – loads up his stock prior to setting off on his rounds of door-to-door selling

coming on the internal railway from the auction. These bunches are specially tailored to suit the taste of the country where they will be sold. Red and white bunches are popular in Germany, and shades of pink have recently been the top seller in France, while the English apparently prefer lots of different colours mixed together. Some firms even design a new bouquet every month and advertise their 'bunch of the month' in the various countries with which they deal. Each bunch comes already wrapped, so the florist only has to stand it in a bucket in the shop and wait for someone to buy it.

THE TULIP STORY

Flowers, particularly bulbs, are big business to the Dutch – and not just as cut flowers; they are the backbone of the tourist trade. Each year thousands of visitors from all over the world visit Holland to see the bulbfields in bloom. But not all the tulips and daffodils are grown to be cut for flowers. Some bulbs are grown for selling as bulbs, for gardeners to plant in their own gardens. To make sure of growing the biggest bulbs, which fetch the best price, growers will cut the flowers off rather than let plants waste their energy going to seed. Instead of just throwing the flowers away, they are made into vividly coloured carnival-style floats at one or other of the bulb festivals. Although these occasions are high on the list of tourist pullers, you don't have to go all the way to Holland to see one. English bulb growers around Spalding in Lincolnshire hold a festival, too.

Another big tourist attraction is the Keukenhof Gardens, famous for its spring bulb extravaganza. As well as seeing masses of bulb flowers of all kinds, naturalized and in formal borders, you can also learn here how to arrange them. Demonstrations feature regularly during the bulb season, leaving tourists certain that, whatever else they take back with them, a bag of Dutch bulbs will be on their shopping list.

The bulb for which Holland is best known is of course the tulip. If we think bulbs are big business nowadays, back in the seventeenth century they were even more so. 'Tulipomania' was the horticultural equivalent of the South Sea Bubble. Speculators made and lost fortunes virtually overnight. It all started when merchants started sailing overseas, bringing back new and exotic plants as well as goods for trade. Flower growing became an extremely popular and fashionable pastime, and wealthy collectors were prepared to pay large sums for the one-upmanship value of owning rare and newly discovered plants. Tulips, originally from the mountainous areas of Turkey and parts of Tibet, were grown at a few exclusive gardens in Europe – until one of the growers moved to Holland, taking his precious tulip bulbs with him. Dutch collectors clamoured for tulips, with their large and colourful flowers, and the man who introduced them was smart enough to recognize the potential of the situation. He sold some of his bulbs to fellow enthusiasts – at enormous prices. The new growers in turn bred and interbred their new plants, selling the offspring at the same inflated prices in what was a real seller's market.

What really caused most of the trouble was that, somewhere along the line, a mutation had crept in. Instead of remaining single-coloured flowers, as nature intended, the mutation produced all sorts of freakish, streaked, multicoloured flowers. It was thought to have been caused by a virus that made the colour 'break', but whatever it was collectors absolutely raved over them. There were several distinct kinds, named according to the different kinds of 'break' – bizzares were yellow tulips with red streaks, and bicolours were white with pink or mauve streaks.

The craze lasted three years, from 1634 to 1637. During this time tulip bulbs were literally worth their weight in gold. A few pounds of bulbs of one rare variety were sold for 500 florins and a coach and horse. Another merchant paid 3000 guilders for a particularly rare and expensive bulb – just one – which he left on his desk while he went out. When he came back he found it was missing – a sailor passing through the office had mistaken it for an onion and eaten it for his work.

People bought all the tulips they could possibly afford and planted them, gambling that a new 'break' would turn up and make them a fortune. Those who couldn't afford them simply pawned everything they owned to buy the bulbs. But suddenly, instead of continually spiralling upwards, prices began to drop. Immediately everyone wanted to sell their investments before they got their fingers burnt – and there were plenty who did, even so.

But the funny thing about it all is that nowadays the 'broken' tulips have virtually vanished from cultivation. Just about the last place where you can see them now is the Hortus Bulborum near Limmen in Holland, a sort of living museum of old flower bulb varieties. They are in flower during April, so if you plan a visit to the bulbfields why not add them to your itinerary?

CONTINENTAL-STYLE ARRANGING

So just what is the continental style? The Continent, of course, consists of several countries, each of which has its own individual approach. But, as a very general rule, all the Continentals make much more use of foliage than we do; the English style depends on masses of flowers, and traditionally we don't see why we should pay good money for leaves at a florist's. And since on the Continent flowers are bought from the florist, not picked from the garden as ours very often are, perhaps one reason they use them sparingly is simply economy – foliage is cheaper than flowers. But the flowers they do use, as I mentioned earlier, tend to be rather more special – look at all the luscious tropical exotics you find there in place of the cottage garden flowers we English traditionally favour.

Four flowers sold on the continent and often used in arrangements, but seldom seen in this country: *top left and right*, gypsophila and banksja; *bottom, left and right*, bird of paradise (strelitzia) and alium

And whereas our garden flowers look better in bulk than individually, those exotic varieties need a bit of space and a good background to set them off to best advantage.

The other big difference between continental and English styles is the vases. In English arrangements the vase is there to hold water, and that is the end of the story. But on the Continent design is very much more important,‚ and the container plays a big part. Your perfect dinner party guest, ordering his thank-you gift at a florist's, will as likely as not specify the kind of container as well as the kind of flowers. And just as there are changing fashions in flowers, colours and arranging styles, so there are changing fashions in containers. Recently the favourite Dutch vases were plain white in colour

A Norwegian-style arrangement which shows their strong feeling for natural growth. Like the German, this type of design has a firm central line, but a softer edge. In Norway they tend to use dried material a great deal, because fresh flowers are not so readily available. *Arranged by Michael Saunders*

and low in profile. The next fashion could be anybody's guess.

But to get away from the generalities, and look at what's what in specific countries, you need to realize why there is so much difference between what is done in countries which are, after all, joined together with good road and rail links.

It all comes back to this business of climate. The further north you go, the colder it gets and the more expensive it becomes to grow flowers under glass. You can always import them from Holland, but the cost of transport is high. Cheap, bulky flowers are not worth the expense, whereas the pricier exotics are. So in Scandinavian countries they tend to use for their 'best' arrangements lots of driftwood and similar material, with just a few very special flowers. The rest of the time, they often make do with dried flowers.

Conversely, the further south you go, the warmer it gets and the more fashionable is patio pot gardening outdoors. In this kind of climate flowers grow so well outdoors, provided they can be kept watered, that there is little need to bring in a lot of expensive flowers from elsewhere, and people tend to use whatever is available locally. Colours, as mentioned earlier,

In this Scandinavian-style arrangement, the elements of the design follow the natural line of growth of the flowers and other materials used in its composition. The low-level interest is characteristic, as is the use of moss and pebbles along with the piece of pine, lily of the valley and alium which form the focus of interest. *Arranged by Michael Saunders*

tend to vary according to the national character – hard, bright colours go down best in Germany, soft pastels are tops in France, while just about anything, so long as it is new and adventurous, will be a winner in Holland.

PECULIARLY CONTINENTAL FLORAL PHENOMENA

Pot-et-fleur arrangements

A rather unusual method of using flowers which is thought to have originated on the Continent is the pot-et-fleur. As its name suggests, it consists of a combination of potted plants and cut flowers in a single arrangement. It is a nice idea, because it means that you can combine a semi-permanent arrangement of plants with an ever-changing sequence of different cut flowers, thus ringing the changes without a major upheaval.

Pot-et-fleur arrangements are very easy to do. The plant part is just the same as making up a bowl garden. You need a large bowl without draining holes in the bottom – an old porcelain washbasin would be ideal. Put some bits of broken pot or clean gravel in the bottom, and fill to just beneath the brim with potting compost. Next, work out the most attractive way of arranging your plants, tip them out of their pots and pop them in place. Most house plants can be used in pot-et-fleurs, but it is important to plant together only those that need a very similar amount of light and water. In general, foliage plants chosen for striking leaf shapes and textures look best in pot-et-fleurs, as they make such a good background for the flowers to come. Specially recommended are weeping fig (*Ficus benjamina*), ivies, coloured-leafed begonias, castor oil plant (*Fatsia japonica*), ferns – bird's nest, maidenhair and Boston, yucca, umbrella plant (*Cyperus*), kangaroo vine and palms. You could add one or two plants with coloured leaves such as croton, fittonia, maranta or calathea, but flowering plants should be avoided as they detract from the flower arrangement, and in any case need replacing when their flowers finish.

Now you are ready for some flowers. Putting them dead-centre looks a little contrived; off-centre or even well to one side looks far better. The vase need not be anything special – just something to hold water. A jam jar would be fine, as you won't see it anyway. Sink it into the compost between the plants, and arrange the flowers in it. Rather than aiming at any particular style of arrangement, the trick is to make the flowers harmonize well with the pot plants. The flowers should look so natural that you might almost think they were growing there. To help the illusion, choose flowers that look the right size for the plants, and try to get tropical-looking flowers to go with exotic plants, and vice versa. For a really sophisticated touch, use flowers that pick out a colour in your foliage plants. Or add to the finished bowl a small figurine, a piece of cork bark or rock to create an extra point of interest.

Hand bunches

The continental florist's 'hand bunch' is not only a very practical way of giving flowers, it is also a very useful way of doing flowers for the home.

If you are picking flowers from your own garden, you can arrange them in one hand as you walk round. Nor do you need to bother with floral foam or pinholders – the flowers hold themselves in place. A hand bunch is a very quick and easy way of making an informal arrangement designed to be seen from all round, so it is perfect for a family table centre or to go on a coffee table. This is how it's done:

Start with the flower that will be at the centre of the bunch; this should be the tallest one. Hold it in your left hand, and make the next flowers form a ring round it. Each successive ring of flowers needs to be slightly shorter than the last. Turn the arrangement round all the time to keep it symmetrical (see drawing 2 opposite). When your bunch is big enough, tie a piece of not-too-thick string tightly round the stems, and just

Making a continental-style 'hand bunch'

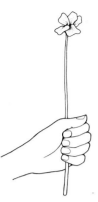

Start with the tallest flower, which
will be the centre of the
arrangement

Add progressively
shorter flowers
around the outside,
turning the bunch in
your hand as you do
so

It is important to add new flowers
with their stems overlapping each
other at an angle, so that the
finished bunch 'relaxes' into an
informal arrangement rather than
looking too much like a florist's
bunch of flowers

To finish off, bind the stems with
string or cotton – or, as a florist
would, with an elastic band. Hook
one end of the elastic band over a
strong stem, then wind it around
the bunch of stems a couple of
times, and hook the other end of the
band over another strong stem

drop the bunch into a suitable sized vase. To make an even
more secure hand bunch tie the end of the string to the stem of
your first flower, and bind each ring of flowers in place with a
turn of string before going onto the next. Once the
arrangement is made up, you cannot replace odd flowers that
wither as you could if you had been using floral foam or a
pinholder. But on the other hand, changing the water is no
trouble at all. Just lift out the whole arrangement, and drop it
back into clean water.

Arranging bulb flowers

On the Continent, where they grow bulbs by the hundreds of acres, there is nothing unusual about the idea of using them as cut flowers. But in Britain we don't do very much with them. This seems a little strange, when you consider what popular garden plants they are.

Part of the problem stems from our natural gardeners' thrift – we don't like buying flowers that we've got growing in the garden, and we don't like cutting the daffs and tulips because they last longer outdoors. But as much of the reason, I'm sure, is that we are not entirely sure what to do with them or how to make then last – so we avoid using them because we think they are difficult. Take tulips for instance. You buy them, arrange them – and next minute they are flopping all over the place, almost as if they have minds of their own. And, daffodils seem to kill any other flowers that you put with them.

Given a few simple tips, however, bulb flowers can be used in the same ways that you would any other flowers, on their own or in mixed arrangements with other kinds. And the same tips apply whether you are buying flowers or cutting them from your own garden.

1. Don't buy, or cut, bulb flowers while they are in tight bud, especially if they are still green with no colour showing. This is especially important for tulips. They won't last longer; rather the reverse, they might not open at all. Choose ones that are just starting to open instead.
2. Get them into water fast, and recut the stems under water to prevent an airlock forming. If bought from a shop, don't worry about cutting several inches off the bottom of the stem – it isn't a waste, it will actually help them last longer. It isn't necessary to arrange them at this stage; just leave them in a bucket of water until you are ready.
3. Use something to keep the water clean; it is worth using on all bulb flowers the special flower-life extender for tulips, but if you can't get any simply add a capful of bleach to each gallon of water.
4. Wash the slimy sap away from cut daffodil stems until they don't ooze any more, and keep them in a bucket of their own until you have done so. After that they can perfectly safely be mixed with other flowers.
5. Forget the old wives' tales about how to stop tulips drooping; making a pinhole through the stem under the flower head doesn't help, and wiring, which is often advised, takes ages. Just make sure their stems are cut short under water so that there is no chance of an air bubble forming inside, and change their water regularly so the stems don't get stopped up.

HOW CONTINENTAL FLOWER ARRANGING BEGAN

As we saw earlier, flower arranging does not mean the same thing to the Continentals as it does to us, not least because the

continental housewife like to receive her flowers after they
have already been arranged for her. This is rather funny really,
when you think that the art of flower arranging originally came
from the Continent.

Of course, since way back people have been putting flowers
in containers of some sort without making anything special of
it. But it was a reasonably hit-or-miss affair; nobody thought of
arranging them in any special way until flower paintings
became all the rage, and artists who didn't think the normal
jumble of flowers looked very nice composed their pictures in
such a way as to show the flowers off better. Flower arrangers
later copied what they did, and their ideas became the basis of
flower arranging – English style – as we know it today.

It all started back in seventeenth-century Holland. After
many hundreds of years, during which the Church had
dominated the arts and religious paintings were the main
output of artists who wanted to sell their work, a new
moneyed class arose. Overseas trade meant that some of the
merchants and businessmen had made considerable fortunes
– and, not suprisingly, were looking around for things to
spend their money on. It fast became all the rage, as described
earlier, to have large collections of the new and rare plants
continually arriving from abroad, such as tulips. The new rich
also took over from the Church as large-scale buyers of art. Not
unnaturally, they wanted to buy paintings that reflected their
new status in society and their new interests. Artists turned to
portraits, still lifes – and flower paintings. Paintings which
featured all the latest in fashionable new plants were all the
more desirable – which is why you see so many packed with
tulips, the status symbol of the moment.

One group of artists cornered the market in flower painting,
estabishing a popular style in which flowers are shown massed
together in bouquets against a plain, uncluttered background.
Three Flemish artists, 'Velvet' Breughel, Ambrosius
Bosschaert and De Gheyn, became the only people to study
under if you wanted to make your mark as an artist, and
predictably the style they started was very much copied. But it
wasn't for another few years yet that Van Aelst appeared on
the scene. He was probably the first artist to introduce a
definite shape to his 'arrangements'. Instead of copying the
vaguely oval outline and symmetrical arrangement of earlier
artists' bouquets, he used asymmetrical designs with a strong
'line' running through – a sloping S shape, later popularized
by Hogarth and misnamed the Hogarth curve. This sort of
arrangement has been the foundation of English-style flower
arranging ever since.

If you look at any of the famous flower paintings of the
period, one thing may strike you as a little bit odd. All those
different flowers would never have been in bloom at the same
time. The reason for depicting them in this way is that artists
did not paint from a real bouquet in front of them, but rather
they would design one from a series of artists' notes which

they had made beforehand. A hundred years or so before flower paintings became so fashionable, artists already were painting flowers, but individual specimens, in water colours, which were used by nurserymen's travelling salesmen almost as catalogues to help them sell plants to their customers. Artists continued the habit of doing these plant 'portraits', using them to piece together larger works later.

Another thing that often strikes us as rather strange about some of these famous flower paintings is that they contain all sorts of objects apparently unconnected with flowers, such as skulls, hourglasses with the sand running out, rotting apples, lizards, frogs and insects. But far from being a reflection of current home decorating trends, it was just the artist indulging himself in a little symbolism. Back in the days when the Church controlled the arts, painters were required to use plenty of symbolic representation. Flowers were used not just as pretty decorations, but to represent hidden meanings. Portraits of the Virgin Mary, for instance, rarely failed to include a madonna lily, which symbolized purity. And just because a different class of people had taken over the arts, artists saw no reason to lose this added attraction to their work. Flower paintings were a marvellous vehicle for symbolism of the more morbid sort – all those rotting fruits, lizards and insects were supposed to be humbling reminders of man's short stay on earth, of death and decay. One artist in particular made a positive fetish of it – if you look at the work of De Savery, it doesn't come as much of a surprise to discover that he ended his life in an asylum for the insane. Of course, not all flower artists were such purveyors of doom and gloom. Some would paint a bird's nest filled with eggs alongside their vase of flowers instead, as an emblem of resurrection, an altogether more cheerful concept.

By the later seventeenth and early eighteenth century, flower painting was an obsession in the art world. It also went through some subtle changes of style; up to the mid-seventeenth century flowers were painted to look as natural as possible. Later, as gardening and plant collecting, became the chief pastime of wealthy aristocrats, artists were commissioned to record their patrons' collections in almost botanical detail.

In the early nineteenth century, one of the keenest of the garden and plant enthusiasts was the Empress Josephine of France, who laid out the famous garden at Malmaison, employing the now famous artist Redouté to record her treasures there. Her particular favourites were roses, and reproductions of his paintings even today are regular favourites as prints, on table mats and in many other contexts.

3 The Japanese Style

What makes it so different?

To us Westerners, the Japanese are particularly fascinating people. Not only do they live on the other side of the world, eat raw fish and seaweed, and make transistor radios and cars that cost half as much and work twice as well as ours, but they live in houses with paper walls and no furniture, they sit on the floor, and they have funny flower arrangements with secret meanings, made of dead twigs and not much else. Those are the rumours, anyway – and those of us who have never been there are quite happy to go on imagining that things are really like that.

The truth is that Japanese society is indeed very different from ours, but it is a very modern, industralized society in which much of the old tradition has been continued in a form that lets it blend with the new, Westernized way of life. And that includes flower arranging, dead twigs and all, because flower arranging plays an important part in the Japanese way of life. A girl's education isn't complete without it. Companies run courses for their employees, and everywhere you go in Japan you will see flower arrangements in offices, factories and shops, as well as in the home.

It is much more than just a means of decoration, though; Japanese flower arranging has spiritual connotations which drive from its early origins as a temple art, when it was practised by men – priests. It is seen as being one of the paths to enlightenment, and as such taken very seriously indeed over there. Whereas with others kinds of flower arranging it is the finished result that matters, with the Japanese style the way you go about it is just as important. Even the best Japanese flower arranger is not considered to have mastered the subject unless he or she studied the history, theory and philosophy behind the subject, as well as the practical aspects.

If all that makes you think it sounds unnecessarily complicated, don't believe it. Japanese flower arranging travels well. You can learn it in Britain, taking it as seriously or

An arrangement of the *Enshu* school. This particular style is known as a *Kabuwaki*, meaning a double root arrangement, and dates back to the sixteenth century. The iris and willow were first arranged separately in different containers, and then placed in this antique *sunabachi. Arranged by Tineka Robertson*

A typical room in a Japanese inn, with its flower arrangement

An arrangement in the modern freestyle manner, made with New Zealand flax, orchids, Fatsia leaves and gypsophila in a contemporary ceramic container. In freestyle arrangements, plant material is used in a way similar to that in which it grows in nature, in contrast with the abstract style where it is not.
Arranged by Takashi Sawano

otherwise as you want. It looks quite at home in both modern and traditional British homes, even if you don't go into the philosophy behind it. And it is quite extraordinarily therapeutic – as good as a trip to the hairdresser's any day.

As you can see, Japanese arrangements are very different from those we are used to. They include lots of spaces between things, very few flowers, and lots of funny shapes. Why?

Well, – why not? Japan is, after all, right on the other side of the world. It would be strange if their idea of flower arranging was anything like ours. It's all a question of culture and heritage. And theirs is certainly very different from ours.

Japanese flower arranging, the historical background

The origins of the Japanese style of flower arranging, ikebana, can be traced back to the custom of offering branches from trees at Shinto shrines where it became a priestly duty to prolong their life by arranging the branches in vases in the shrine.

When Buddhism reached Japan in the sixth century, the custom of offering flowers to Buddha was brought with it from China. Thus the earliest flower arrangers were priests and the first schools of ikebana were established in temples. The earliest of these is the Ikenobo school founded by Ono-no-Imoko, Head Priest of the Rokkakudo Temple in Kyoto early in the seventh century.

As elsewhere, the state and the established religion were closely linked and so it was a natural development that, in time, ikebana should be taken up by the ruling classes and practised by men of aristocratic birth. Illustrated texts were produced and ikebana was frequently depicted in Japanese art, on painted screens and in woodblock prints.

Incidentally, the term 'ikebana' is relatively modern, only coming into use comparatively recently. The earlier term is Ka-Dō, meaning 'the Way of Flowers', for the practice of ikebana was seen as one of the many 'paths' that could lead one, through personal and spiritual development, to enlightenment.

Two seemingly contradictory tastes are seen in ikebana, as in most other forms of Japanese art. One is for gorgeous colours, intricate and elaborate designs. Examples of this are the *Rikka* or landscape style, for which formal rules were laid down in the twelfth century, and much modern free-style work. The other taste is for the austere and simple and shows the influence of Zen. This encapsulates what many Westerners regard as 'the true feeling of Japan'. The *Seika* or *Shoka* style which developed in the sixteenth century and where often only a single type of branch is used, is representative of this tradition, as is the simplicity of *Chabana* (Tea flowers). Chabana was created by Sen-no-Rikkyu, the great Tea Master who simplified and refined the Tea Ceremony in the sixteenth century and established the form most widely practised today.

Up until the middle of the nineteenth century the most important masters and practictioners of ikebana were men. These were not, as some people might imagine, effete aesthetes. Samurai, after a hard day on the battlefield, would relax and regain their *wa* (inner harmony) by practising *Cha-Dō* (the Way of Tea) and creating an ikebana arrangement. Geisha were expected to be able to do ikebana, but it was not until after the Meiji Restoration when Japan opened its doors to the West in 1867, when women were encouraged to enter fields formerly reserved for men, that ikebana began to be widely practised by them. Nowadays most Japanese women study ikebana in one of the many hundreds of schools that now exist, at some time in their lives. But even today many of the great masters of the art are men.

In a traditional Japanese room the predominant colours are soft browns and muted golds and there is only one place where decoration may be put. This is the *tokonoma*, an alcove usually 1 metre (3 ft) deep and 2 metres (6 ft) high and wide. Here a scroll hangs, on it a ink-painting or beautifully written poem on a theme in keeping with the season or the occasion. To the right or the left of the scroll is an arrangement, made to complement the scroll. This explains many aspects of traditional ikebana. All the material leans forward towards the viewer because the arrangement could only be seen from the front and the arrangement is asymmetric to make a balance with the scroll. When ikebana moved out of the *tokonoma* a revolution took place.

Japan's response to Western influence was, as we all know phenomenal. Ikebana, too, adapted itself to changes in architecture and life-style. Since the beginning of the twentieth century many new Schools of ikebana have grown up and new styles have been created incorporating exotic plants and flowers from other countries, and materials such as driftwood, metal and even paper and plastic. Ikebana itself has been taken abroad where it is increasingly wisely studied and encouraged through such organisations as Ikebana International.

It isn't really as odd as it looks

The English style of flower arranging, as mentioned earlier, reflects very closely our gardens outdoors, with flowers everywhere – masses of them, all crammed close together, then so does the Japanese. Their flower arranging styles also follow their gardening styles. It's just that their garden are very different from what we now normally recognise as such.

Proper Japanese gardens are not based on trees, shrubs or lawns, still less the barbecues, sandpits and hordes of kids playing football that make up the average British family garden. To the Japanese, the garden is a retreat from the world

A Japanese garden – a small piece of the natural landscape tamed and tidied so that it becomes a perfect retreat from the everyday world

where you can quietly contemplate the beauties of nature. And instead of lots of distracting colours and flowers that keep changing, the Japanese garden is very meticulously planned to resemble a piece of natural landscape, with rocks, shale, gnarled and stunted trees apparently sculpted by the wind, an occasional flower strategically sited, a pool with a lantern. It is designed to save you the bother of having to find your own mountaintop to sit on; you simply construct one outside the back door. Far from being as un-natural as it sounds to us, that is exactly what the wild places of Japan look like. All the Japanese have done is rebuild a tidied up bit where they want it – which is no different from what we do, really. The average English garden is, after all, has lawns instead of fields, and ornamental trees, roses and shrubs instead of bushes, briars and copses. And while we find it mildly therapeutic to mow the lawn and wash the car on a Sunday, the Japanese gardener gets the same benefit from raking his gravel into patterns like waves on the seashore.

So Japanese gardening and flower arranging, as in other countries, go hand in glove. But that is only part of the story. Nature means much more to the Japanese than a place to run the dog or have a picnic. It is literally a religion. Shinto, the oldest Japanese religion, worships nature and treats all forms of life, however humble, with the very greatest of respect. Japanese flower arranging has its roots in that same Shinto religion. And since they regarded all life as sacred – even plants – the early priests never cut more than they really needed, and took great care to make it last as long as possible. Although Japanese flower arranging has been through many changes of style since the early temple days, those basic principles still hold good today. Modern styles continue to use an absolute minimum of material strategically positioned for maximum effect, and proper care of cut flowers is still strongly advocated. So one of the reasons why Japanese flower arrangements contain such as lot of empty space is a concern for conserving nature.

The Japanese have a very different idea from the Western eye on what constitutes beauty – which in turn has a bearing on the way they choose to arrange their flowers. In the West, we find things aesthetically pleasing and therefore beautiful if they are symmetrical, or at least reasonably so. And we like beautiful things in quantity. The Japanese, on the other hand, find asymmetrical design more attractive, and they prefer beauty to be understated – they like to be able to appreciate a single object and understand it completely, rather than have their attention distracted by too much all at once. Shapes and the spaces between them are almost as important as the objects themselves. You have only got to look at Japanese painting and other art forms to see what I mean, but that philosophy applies equally to Japanese gardens and flower arrangements. The preference for underplaying the arts seems to originate once again from the old Shinto religion, which practised restraint in all things. In their temple arrangements they preferred foliage to flowers, which is one reason why Japanese arrangements even today rely very heavily on branches and leaves, including only a few flowers.

Apart from the sparseness and lack of symmetry of Japanese arrangements, they exhibit one more feature that makes them look rather strange to us – perhap 'look' isn't quite the right word for it, because it's more like a vaguely uncomfortable feeling which you can't quite put your finger on. What it comes down to is that your eye, instead of being led into a nice safe focal point somewhere near the middle, as in English arrangements, keeps finding itself led right out of the arrangement. The fact is that in Japanese flower arrangements the focal point isn't inside the arrangement at all. *You*, the onlooker, are the focal point. The result is the slightly eerie feeling that, instead of you looking at the flowers, they are actually looking at you!

What about the secret meanings Japanese flower arranging is supposed to possess? There is certainly a lot of symbolism in the flowers and plants chosen, and the basic layout of the arrangement itself. But there is no need to get too alarmed by it – we actually do much the same thing with our own style of flower arranging, without really being aware of it. For instance, we use certain flowers at Christmas or Easter; some flowers automatically make you think of spring, while leaves on the turn put you in mind of autumn. Some flowers could be used to suggest good luck – white heather and shamrocks, for example. Pumpkins remind one of Halloween. And so on; there are plenty of examples you could think of.

The Japanese style use certain foliage and flowers which have the same sort of connotations to them. It only seems strange to us because the plants are unfamiliar in the particular context – a kind of small bamboo suggests luck to them; they don't grow white heather or shamrock, but the bamboo grows everywhere. Cherry and plum blossom, pine and bamboo are commonly used in Japanese arrangements because they all grow plentifully. It's no different from us using dahlias or roses. But of course, now that Western flowers are also grown in Japan, you find them being used in modern arrangements too.

Japanese arrangements normally have three main 'lines' which represent heaven, earth and man and the relationship between them. If you study Ikebana – which is the proper name for the whole concept of Japanese flower arranging – in depth the symbolic aspects will probably become very important – but there are many people in Britain who learn Japanese flower arranging just because they like the look of it and enjoy doing it.

A Seika arrangement of the *Enshu* school, which dates from the fifteenth century. This arrangement is made of a single apple branch, which has been very skilfully bent into the shape you see here by inserting many minute wedges cut from another branch with a saw; this design contains a total of twenty wedges. The container is an antique bronze *usubata*. *Arranged by Tineka Robertson*

Above top left, A traditional English pedestal arrangement. *Arranged by John Wareing*

Above top right, A Victorian-style table-centre arrangement of roses and foliage for a formal dinner. *Arranged by Pamela South*

Right, An English Art Nouveau-style arrangement of lilies with peacock feathers, whose graceful, flowing line echoes that of the accompanying figurine. *Arranged by Pamela South*

A German-style arrangement, which shows well their strong, clear line. Flowers are used in the way they would naturally grow, with those that need most room at the top. Here, the flowers used include astromeria, wallflower, liatris, cinneraria, roses, lily of the valley and bluebells. *Arranged by Michael Saunders*

The final stages of producing a Dutch Christmas arrangement using cut amaryllis. Also forming a setting for the candle are roses, South African foliage and conifer foliage *By courtesy of the Flower Council of Holland*

Takashi Sawano with his arrangement of New Zealand flax (*Phormium*), gypsophilia, fatsia leaves, orchids and driftwood. In a modern ceramic container, this is a freestyle arrangement

A moon-shaped container with apple blossom, an arrangement of the seventeenth-century *Enshu* school. The Japanese call this a *tsuribana* – meaning hanging – arrangement. The monkeys which form part of the chain are supposed to pull the moon out of the water. *Arranged by Tineke Robertson*

An upright Ikebana arrangement of pine and chrysanthemums with apple blossom, a *Rikka* arrangement of the sixteenth-century *Ikenobo* school. The idea here is to recreate a piece of the natural Japanese landscape in a vase, using the same sort of materials that occur in nature. *Arranged by Tineke Robertson*

A 6-foot high abstract arrangement inspired by modern sculpture, made of bleached ivy stems, wood base veneer, and lilies.
Arranged by Pamela South

An abstract arrangement made to stand on the floor, based in a hollow tree stump, with lilies and stems of Solomon's seal from which most of the leaves have been removed to reveal the flowers.
Arranged by Pamela South

Left, a colourful swag of preserved flowers designed for a flower festival. The flowers used include hollyhock, anemone, statice and dahlias *Arranged by Maureen Foster*

Below, an elegant preserved flower arrangement of white hollyhocks, shrubby spiraea and feverfew, interspersed with a few ferns *Arranged by Maureen Foster*

Artificial trees made
from moss and a section
of tree branch set in a
'nest' style container of
natural twigs filled with
more moss. *Arranged by
Kenneth Turner*

An arrangement of
dried flowers in a
basket, very simple but
incredibly effective.
*Arranged by Kenneth
Turner*

Learning Ikebana

While you could teach yourself a sort of Japanese-look flower arranging at home from a book, that's about all it would be. To learn properly you need a teacher and a class. That way, as well as finding out about the authentic Ikebana, you will also have a lot of enjoyment, make some new friends, and discover an entirely new means to relax. Some people learning Ikebana at classes say that since taking it up they no longer suffer from tension headaches and other stress-related problems. The Ikebana Trust, whose address can be found at the back of this book, run classes at their rooms in London, but they should be able to put you in touch with classes elsewhere in Britain too. Other classes are sometimes available at the Royal Horticultural Society, also in London.

In Japan, there was traditionally a lot more to being a flower arranging teacher than just teaching flower arranging. The teacher was the person to whom pupils confided their problems: a sort of agony aunt – or uncle. Some tutors even used to do a little matchmaking on the side, and many Japanese met their future partners through introductions arranged by the tutor.

Not all teachers of Ikebana belong to the same 'school' or style. In ancient Japan, whenever a student had a major disagreement on technique with his tutor he would go off and start a new school of flower arranging based on his particular ideas of how it should be done. Since, over the centuries, popular styles of Ikebana have changed anyway, it is not surprising that different people favour different styles.

Even nowadays some people teach a very formal school, while others teach the Ikebana of a much more modern school. If you are going to learn properly, visit some exhibitions of the different kinds first, so that you can attach yourself to the school whose style you like best.

Ikebana is one of those subjects you can keep on learning for years, and it has a lot in common with learning karate – the student learns a series of set pieces, and progresses from one level of instruction to another. You don't actually get a black belt for flower arranging, but you can periodically be awarded a certificate when your tutor thinks you have achieved a certain level of proficiency; some schools will even award you a Japanese name.

You might think that learning set pieces would take all the imagination and initiative out of flower arranging, but it doesn't. A class of half a dozen students, each learning to make one of the basic styles, would end up with six very different-looking arrangements, even though they all used the same 'set' formula. In fact, the very fact that beginners do have a formula to work to makes it that much easier for them to get to grips with the subject. Instead of you having to worry about whether this branch will look better here or somewhere else, and whether that stem should be longer or shorter, each arrangement has its own plan to follow. There are rules governing the length of all the three main 'lines' – heaven, earth and man – based on the height or width of the container, and laying down the angles at which you place the three lines. This takes all the worry out of the task, leaving you to concentrate on choosing your materials, trimming them in the way you want, and deciding what else to use as a filler-in between the three main lines; in other words, to contemplate nature, which is what it's all about.

Once you have spent some time learning the basics, you might progress to free-style arrangements. Here you are free to do your own thing flower-wise, especially if you study one of the modern schools.

Ikebana Gadgetry

Because Ikebana is so very different from other sorts of flower arranging you will not be surprised to learn that a whole sub-culture of gadgets exists, peculiar to this particular form of the art. That does not mean to say that it is particularly expensive to take up Ikebana, because everything you need for use in classes will be lent to you by your tutor. And if you want to practise at home, you can make do perfectly well with everyday things around the kitchen and garden shed. But let's look at some of the special Japanese equipment.

First of all we'll examine things to hold your flowers in place. There is no Japanese equivalent of Oasis, but they do use what they call Kenzan, which are actually pinholders. These are more heavyweight than the usual kind, first because they very often have to counterbalance the weight of branches hanging over to one side of the arrangement, and secondly because the pins are usually rather stronger, in order to cater for all the tough, woody material they are called upon to prong. You can buy proper Japanese Kenzan from the Ikebana Trust (there's a discount for members), but alternatively you could get by reasonably well using the stoutest pinholder you can find, plasticined down hard into the bottom of your container. If it still overbalances, try weighting down the container with pebbles. In the more formal Japanese flower arranging schools they use small, forked wooden twigs between which the flowers are wedged but this is rather a specialized business, so do not try it yourself until you have seen it demonstrated.

At Ikebana classes, special scissors called Hasami are used, which become as much a part of their owner as a 'best' pair of secateurs to a keen gardener. They are actually rather like a cross between toenail clippers and secateurs, but without the spring-loaded action. They are sufficiently rugged to cut with precision all the gnarled, woody stems you are every likely to use. More of them get lost with the rubbish after a class than

A modern vertical freestyle arrangement made with pampus grass, plaited palm leaf, Tokyo chrysanthemums, and elaeagnus foliage. The container is an authentic Ichiyo one from Japan. *Arranged by Bridget Stanley*

ever wear out or break. But again, if you want to improvise at home a good pair of secateurs would do.

Vases are the real problem to the beginner, because the formula for each different set piece Japanese arrangement also specifies the sort of container it should have. Some need wide, shallow containers, others tall, upright ones. Some even need a pair of identical containers for a two-part arrangement. The true Ikebana vases are usually imported from Japan at rather fancy prices – even the ones made in this country tend to be handmade specially for the job, and they are still far more expensive than a standard English-style vase. If you turn out to be a real enthusiast, you'll probably want to acquire your own Japanese vases. But in the meantime you can make do with appropriately sized casserole dishes, deep plates and so on. Usually the teacher will recommend something practical that you can use for a little homework without needing to go to any expense. And of course there is one another incentive to practising at home – Ikebana uses so few flowers that it can actually be cheaper to do than most other kinds of flower arranging.

A simple Ikebana Arrangement*

You will need:

1. A shallow container, either round or rectangular, 10–12 inches wide and 1 1/2–2 inches deep. Choose a plain colour, preferably dark.

2. A pin holder; the proper Japanese pinholder – a heavy duty version of ours, is called a *kenzan*.

3. A pair of secateurs or proper Ikebana scissors which will cut both branches and flower stems.

4. Branches (suggestions; pussy willow privet, dogwood, hornbeam, maple or cotoneaster are easy to work with).

5. Flowers. Ikebana uses very few so it isn't an expensive hobby. For this arrangement you only need 3–5 flowers. (Suggestions; carnations, roses, anemones, daffodils, or dahlias). The flowers should be at different stages of development so include some buds as well as open flowers.

How to measure your container, to establish its size

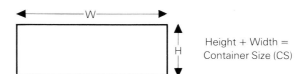

Height + Width = Container Size (CS)

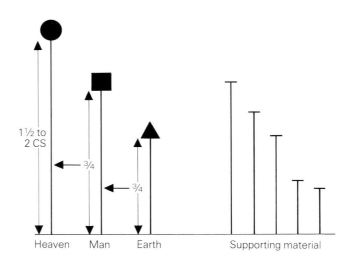

How to measure your material

* This section has kindly been contributed by Elizabeth Palmer.

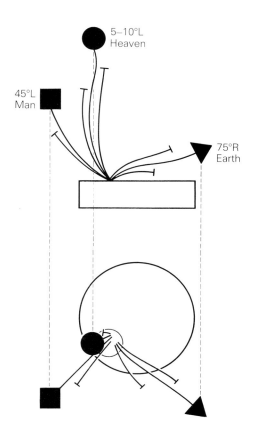

5–10°L
Heaven

45°L
Man

75°R
Earth

Front view of the
arrangement

Bird's eye view of the
arrangement

Position of stems in
the *kenzan*

HOW TO ASSEMBLE

Basic Ikebana arrangements such as this one are made up of three main lines made from branches of flowers, which represent Heaven, Earth and Man.

The length of each 'line', and the angles between them and the vertical, are all laid down in what amounts to a recipe. The following series of drawings sets this out for you. Although you might think six people following the same 'pattern' would come up with six identical arrangements, they don't. Try it for yourself, using different mixes of flowers and branches each time, and see.

First, place the pinholder in the container towards the front left-hand side.

Next, cut the three main branches to length – these will be the Heaven, Earth and Man lines. The length of each line depends on the exact size of the container you use; to measure the container for Ikebana purposes, add the width to the height.

The Heaven line (or branch) is longest, it must be 1 1/2–2 times the measurement of your container (width plus height). Measure it roughly by laying the branch over the top of the container, and cut to length with secateurs (see photograph B in the step-by-step sequence). The man line, another branch, is cut about 3/4 the length of the Heaven branch. Earth in this arrangement is represented by a flower in bud, whose stem should be cut so that is 3/4 the length of the Man line.

To begin the arrangement, start with the Heaven line branch, but before placing it onto the pinholder, (see photograph C) spend a moment or two studying it to see which is its best 'side' – this should face the front. Then fix this branch firmly in place on the pinholder, placing it centre back as shown in the photograph. Hold the branch upright, near the base as you fix it in position, and then move it slighlty forward and left so that the tip of the branch is 5–10 degrees from the vertical. Make this adjustment by holding the material near the base, not by pulling the top as this would loosen it. Position this front left as shown in photograph D, overleaf, and after pushing it on the pinholder, incline it forward and left so the tip of the branch finished up 45 degrees from the vertical (see photograph E, overleaf). You will find this business of placing a branch onto the pinholder vertically and then tilting it easiest to do if you cut the bottom off the branch at an angle instead of straight.

The Earth line comes next – the flower bud. This is pushed onto the pinholder front right, as photograph E shows, and it should lean forward to the right at an angle of 75 degrees to the vertical.

To finish off the arrangement, you can now add other flowers up to the maximum permitted in this design of five, and leaves. Although there are no firm instructions in the 'pattern' as to where this extra material should go, there are

A

The type of shallow container most suitable for Ikebana

B

Measuring the Heaven line, or branch

C

Start the arrangement with the Heaven line, or branch

D
Arranging the Man
line, or branch

E
The final position of
the Man line

F

Fixing the Earth line –
in this case the flower
bud – in position

guidelines. Some leaves, for instance, should be used to hide
the pinholder. As well, extra flowers and foliage should
always be placed to follow the direction of one of your three
main lines, which should remain the dominant pieces in the
arrangement. Be careful too not to put material in the space
between the main lines, especially between Heaven and Earth.
This would destroy the essential character of the arrangement
and turn it into a western-style one. Extra material should
always be shorter than the main lines for this same reason.

See photograph G overleaf for the finished arrangement. To
see as it should be seen, put it somewhere in front of a plain,
unpatterned background. Since the arrangement has most of
its material to the left, it should be placed towards the left hand
side of the room or table. If you want an arrangement for the
right hand side of a room, just make a mirror image
arrangement.

The finished design.
*Arranged by Takashi
Sawano*

4   Abstract Flower Arranging

What is it they say about beauty being in the eye of the beholder? Modern art certainly isn't everybody's cup of tea: it takes a bit of understanding to appreciate it fully. But what has it got to do with flower arranging?

The answer is a lot, when you see how the abstract flower arranger has assimilated the theories behind modern art, and used them to create one of the most imaginative and striking styles of flower arranging. And whereas the artist uses unconventional materials such as bits of broken bicycle to make wierd and wonderful shapes of somewhat dubious attraction to the uninitiated, the abstract arranger, using the same guidelines, produces some truly remarkable floral designs which can be appreciated by anyone.

Because the abstract style is so very different from conventional flower arranging, people ofen tend to think it is difficult, and that you have to be an expert arranger before you can tackle it. But although it certainly helps if you already know the basics – how to care for and condition flowers, how to fix them in place with Oasis or a pinholder and so on – it really doesn't matter if you don't have much experience of arranging.

Instead of relying on a few flower arranging rules, the abstract style relies on guidelines derived from the fine arts. It is more like making a work of art – only instead of paint and canvas, clay or stone, you just happen to be using flowers.

If you think the abstract style has more than a little in common with the Japanese one, you wouldn't be far wrong. It originally started out as a kind of Americanized version of Japanese flower arranging. The wives of American servicemen based in Japan after World War II saw Japanese flower arranging and liked it so much that they brought it home with them, adapting it to fit in with a faster pace of life and modern homes. Left to develop in such a different environment from the one in which it had been born and bred , it soon changed almost – but not quite – beyond recognition.

Learning abstract flower arranging

This arrangement is inspired by an idea from Japanese flower arranging (from which the abstract style itself originated) – the use of a pair of matching containers linked together by plant material. *Arranged by Pamela South*

The abstract style uses relatively few flowers with plenty of other accessories to make something that is stylish and eye-catching. In fact it may not use any fresh flowers at all – equally striking results can be achieved using foliage or preserved material. When you look at an abstract arrangement for the first time, you will be struck by the peculiar way the material is used and by some of the odd things used with it. The abstract style does not insist on plant material being used in a natural way – on the contrary, it is generally used in a most unnatural way. So how do you go about learning such a way-out subject?

Given that you already know the rudiments of working with flowers, your main requirement is ideas and a feeling for how to make them work. You can, of course, acquire a lot of ideas from watching demonstrations of abstract flower arranging at flower clubs. But abstract arranging is a very personal business, in which there is no real right and wrong way of doing it. Although you can copy other people's arrangements to give you a 'feel' for the subject, at the end of the day your best ideas come from you.

The only way, short of trial and error, that you can tell what is going to work and what won't is by having a knowledge of fine art and design. Some abstract flower arrangers get so deeply involved that they enrol at evening classes in fine art, a very good way of getting to grips with the subject. But for a start it's a help to know a little of the principles involved.

You don't have to be artistically inclined to make the principles of design work for you – we all do it already without even knowing it. Every time you choose a dress or decorate a room, your subconscious is at work selecting textures that contrast, or colours that harmonize. So let's first of all take an artist's eye view of abstract art and design, and then go on to find out how it will help when it comes to arranging flowers.

WHY ABSTRACT ART?

Representational art is something with which most people feel reasonably happy, because whether they happen to like the subject or not, at least they can see what it is – it's easily recognizable. With abstract art, the subject is just that – abstract. You can't recognize what it is supposed to be. And while some abstract art is loosely based on real objects, but 'mucked about' so that you can't really be sure what they are supposed to be, very often it isn't meant to represent anything at all – it is just a figment of the artist's imagination, and one that is, at least to him or her, aesthetically pleasing.

Looked at like this, all flower arranging is abstract, because we just make an arrangement that looks pretty for its own sake – we don't make arrangements that look like reclining nymphs, portraits of our grandmothers or horses and carts stuck in a stream. The abstract style just looks more abstract than most to someone raised on conventional flower arranging, because of the unique and unconventional ways in which it uses flowers.

But let's get back to abstract art. Because it doesn't present you with any recognizable object, your imagination has to work for its keep. The trick lies in the way the artist uses shapes, colours, and most important, the spaces between them to trigger off responses from your subconscious, making you think of things that aren't depicted at all. For example, in a conventional picture you might see curvy lines as waves along a beach, and jagged ones as mountain peaks. In abstract art, the artist does not cloud the issue by showing you the sea or the mountains – but the same jagged or curvy lines create the identical feeling of calm or danger, even though you can't see the sea or the mountains. Instead of spelling everything out for you at a glance, as conventional art does, abstract art just gives you the bare bones on which to build what you might call your personal daydream.

Artists achieve that effect by using shapes, colours and spaces to establish a series of moods or feelings. Many of the

A 'pop art' abstract arrangement inspired by Andy Warhol's soup cans – a bit of fun for a party arrangement using inexpensive materials. *Arranged by Pamela South*

same principles apply equally well whether your composition is made in paint, scrap iron or flowers; and whether you think of yourself as an artist or a flower arranger.

BALANCE

You know the feeling you get when you see a picture hanging crooked? That uncomfortable must-straighten-it-up feeling is the same sort of reaction we have towards any pattern that looks off-balance. And although a picture may indeed be crooked, the eye can be just as 'put out' by a picture that is hanging perfectly straight – but with a pattern that is visually off-balance. Visual balance is like a trick which our eyes play on us. If you imagine a vertical line drawn through the middle of a design, whether it be a flower arrangement, painting or whatever, you'll see what I mean. In a perfectly symmetrical pattern, both sides of the line will be mirror images of each other. The visual weight is the same each side, so that the eye goes away perfectly happy, although rather quickly bored. An asymmetrical pattern is far more likely to hold the attention; it looks more interesting because each half is completely different. What determines whether the design appears balanced or not is the relative proportions of visually 'light' and 'heavy' material in each half. Light colours and blank spaces look light, and lots of colour and detail look heavy. So to make a design that pleases the eye, even though it is not symmetrical, the artist must balance the amount of light and heavy materials each side of the centre line; a lot of light material one side will balance a little heavy material the other.

In flower arranging terms, we've already seen the idea of visual balance in action with Ikebana. If you remember, the

Japanese prefer their arrangements to be asymmetrical. They make it easy, however, because they have established sets of rules governing each kind of arrangement, to ensure that it is visually balanced. Since the abstract style has its roots in the Japanese one, it's not surprising to find asymmetrical design favoured here too. The big difference is that you have to sort out for yourself what looks balanced and what doesn't.

RHYTHM

Although it is best known as a musical term, rhythm also applies to visual images. Waves on a beach and a field of corn rippling in the wind are both made up of similar shapes with nearly identical spaces between them repreated endlessly. Just like balance, visual rhythm has a comforting effect on the eye looking at it. But having established a nice safe pattern to lull the eye into a sense of security, the artist normally does something pretty abrupt to wake it up again.

CONTRAST AND HARMONY

A contrast is one of those things aimed at waking the eye up, and can be between different colours, textures, shapes or anything else. The intention is always to attract attention.

The other side of the coin is harmony, which means using things together that are very similar in shape, colour or texture. The effect of harmony is much the same as rhythm on the eye looking at it – a nice, safe, lulling-to-sleep pattern. Another musical term, harmony actually has quite a lot in common with rhythm, since it is easy to produce the feeling of either by repeating similar shapes, colours, textures and so on across a design.

Translating rhythm, contrast and harmony into flower arranging isn't difficult; there are lots of flowers of similar shape with which it is possible to create rhythmic patterns or those based on harmonizing shapes or colours. The· daisy family, for instance, has hundreds of members all of very similar shape, but available in various sizes and an almost complete range of colours. Nor is it difficult to create a strong contrast, using a background of harmonizing colours with a point of interest made by a strikingly different shape or colour.

SPACE AND LINE

One of the most striking contrasts is that between an object and the empty space around it, especially if the subject has been carefully choosen to present a spectacular outline. If the shape is enclosed inside a frame of some sort, it will look even more spectacular – the empty space can be as much a part of the design as the objects it surrounds. In both Japanese and abstract flower arranging, the space between individual flowers is as important as the flowers themselves; you don't just arrange flowers, you actually arrange the empty space too.

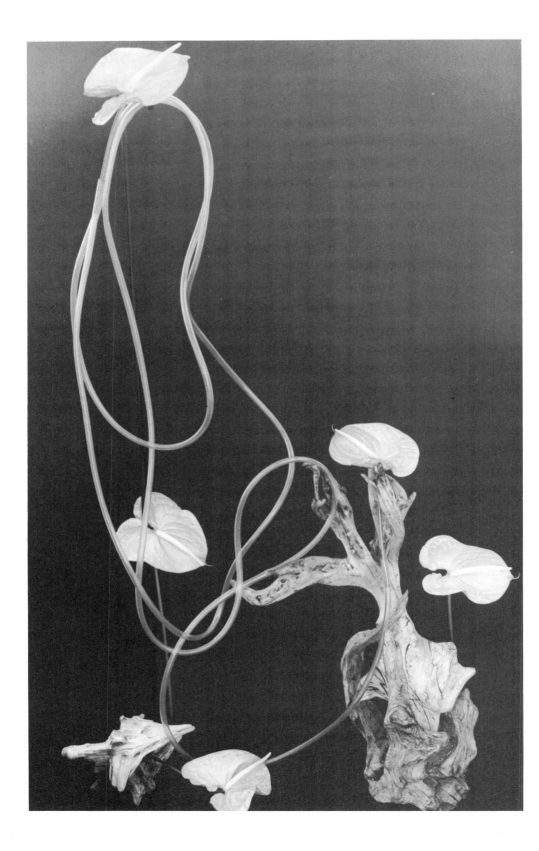

An eye for unusual materials, and knowing how best to use them, are essential to a successful abstract arranger. Here anthurium leaves and driftwood are completed by several yards of plastic pipe! *Arranged by Pamela South*

It is a complete about-face on the traditional English style where, if you can find a bit of space in your arrangement, you shove a flower in quickly before anyone notices.

Line is not quite the opposite of space, but you approach it in a similar way. Flower stems, twigs and so on make natural lines in a way that occurs only infrequently in painting. And even if the line isn't exactly straight, it does achieve the same result by persuading the eye to follow the general direction in which it leads. A collection of lines, alias stems, tends to lead the eye naturally to the focal point of the arrangement, from where they radiate outwards. In the traditional English style, the focal point is always in the lower centre of the arrangement. But in the Japanese and abstract styles it is usually in a different place, and deliberately so. Lines tend to link the points of interest in a design, so in a way they actually lead the eye round it. Without any lines – just a series of unrelated points of interest – the poor old eye would be left wondering where to start first; again, it's another visual trick to make the eye feel at home, and to want more of what it sees.

TEXTURE

If you can imagine a room completely furnished, carpeted and curtained in the same material – let's say velvet – you can imagine visualize how uninteresting it would look, even if all the velvets were different colours and patterns; the texture would be identical everywhere. It's just the same with flower arranging; you need a change of texture to make the finished result look interesting. In flower arranging you have the advantage of a natural break – an unavoidable change of texture between the flowers and the container in which they stand. Beyond that, though, choosing flowers, foliage and accessories with textures that contrast or harmonize, and linking them all to the container, takes some careful thought. It's quite amazing the difference a change of texture can make – you could remake the same arrangement several times, using as your main subject something with a smooth, shiny, rough or prickly texture, and each time completely alter its character. Similarly, a shiny or matt, synthetic or natural container will substantially alter the nature of the arrangement. Finding the right combination of textures can work wonders and really bring an arrangement to life. It's worth practising by holding together differently textured flowers, leaves, containers and accessories such as driftwood to get a good idea of what works best together.

COLOUR

I've left this subject until last, because it's the first thing most people think of when it comes to using flowers. The artist learns a lot more about colour than flower arrangers probably ever need to know, because he is concerned with creating his own colours by mixing them together, whereas the flower arranger just chooses colours from what is available.

If you are seriously interested in the question of colour, get hold of a colour wheel – NAFAS sell one specially for flower arrangers. The wheel is a circle divided into twelve segments, with the three primary colours red, blue and yellow as far apart as they will go; the spaces in between contain the secondary colours green, violet and orange, which the artist makes up by mixing together the primary colours. Between the two come the tertiary colours, which the artist makes by mixing the next-door primary and secondary colours. Since the flower arranger doesn't mix her own colours, this aspect of the colour wheel may seem rather wasted, but it does provided a very useful at-a-glance guide to those colours which harmonize and those that make the most effective contrasts. The trick is that any band of three colours alongside each other on the colour wheel will harmonize, while two colours directly opposite each other give the best contrast. If you don't want such a strong contrast, use the colours on either side of the one directly opposite. Although the colour wheel isn't scientifically based, it does save you a lot of time and thinking.

Choosing flowers and containers that either harmonize or contrast is only the beginning, though. You also have to consider the question of backgrounds. Put the same arrangement in front of half a dozen different backgrounds and you'll see exactly why the right one is so important. Obviously there isn't much point in putting flowers in front of a 'noisy' floral-patterned wallpaper; nor will they be seen at their best in a corner already cluttered with ornaments, nor will a predominantly peach-coloured arrangement be seen to best advantage against a peachy background. To be seen properly against their background, flowers need to contrast with it. Even a neutral background is better than a matching one, but to be really artistic choose a background that picks out one of the minor colours in the arrangement. Actually, although the artist would probably do it this way round, the flower arranger is more likely to do the reverse, choosing flowers to match the existing background rather than redecorate the living room to suit each new arrangement!

Another important aspect of backgrounds is luminosity. In most homes the sort of places where we want to put flowers are often a bit on the dark and dingy side, and if you choose dark or deep-coloured flowers for these places you just won't see them properly. If you stand in a slightly darkened room with half-closed eyes you can see what I mean – the only things you notice are the light-coloured ones. The reverse is also true – in over-bright situations darker-coloured flowers show up best. It's just another instance of contrasting backgrounds.

One of the most interesting ways of playing around with colour is using it to capture the spirit of the occasion. In British society, certain colours have become associated with certain

For the beginner, a simple and effective idea is to make the bare bones of an abstract arrangement from permanent materials like driftwood and gnarled, dried stems, and merely change the living flower element of the design as necessary. Here, the flowers are grouped together at the centre of the arrangement, but you could vary this by grouping a few flowers towards the base of the design, resting in the loop of willow stem, with a single flower in the 'hole' near the top. *Arranged by Pamela South*

events or occasions – red for Christmas, or white for weddings and christenings. And even if you don't enter competitions at flower shows where you have to make an arrangement that interprets the theme of spring or whatever, it's still nice to be able to make arrangements for special occasions that do just that. Spring, for instance, is usually associated with pastel colours – pale yellow and pale pink, such as cowslips and almond blossom; autumn colours are deep oranges, browns and reds, like leaves on the turn. Summer colours are bright yellows, blues and greens, like a sunny sky over a beach or lawn. And winter is white, bare twigs and earth browns.

Developing the art

With all these elements of design, the key lies in developing a sense of 'seeing' things through the eye of an artist. Once you have mastered even the roughest idea of the elements of design, you'll find them cropping up all over the place. Looking for them is a good habit to encourage, as the more ingrained it becomes, the more easily you will be able to arrange flowers. On country walks, for instance, you might notice how a stream makes a contrast against a rough stone bridge, and in town you'll probably find yourself thinking about how well or badly people have chosen their clothes. Like any hobby, it tends to stay with you even when you aren't actually doing it. Certainly it makes life more interesting.

A SHORT CUT

By the time you have played around with abstract flower arranging for a while, the chances are that you will have come up with a few designs that particularly take your fancy. Or perhaps at a demonstration or in a book you will have seen something you liked enough to copy at home. Instead of taking it all to bits when the flowers or leaves die, you could always leave just the bare bones of the arrangement – the driftwood or other non-perishable elements, and put new flowers in. They need not neccesarily be the same kind as the ones you took out; instead try something different and see what effect the change has on the arrangement. You can make a tremendous change just by altering one element; sometimes you would hardly know it was the same arrangement. In fact, there is no reason why you should not keep on adapting old favourites until you have the time to try out something completely different.

ACCESSORIES

In the same way that you gradually develop a talent for spotting the right combinations of flowers, container and background, another requirement will soon make itself apparent when you take to abstract flower arranging. To put the finishing touch to an arrangement successfully you need to be able to spot the hidden potential in unlikely objects plucked from obscurity. All sort of extraordinary things make their appearance in abstract flower arrangements, because flowers are only one part of the total design. Bits of dried wood, lumps of stone, shells, pieces of coral, odds and ends from junk shops, wire netting, bits of chrome and other odd metalwork – just about anything goes where the abstract is concerned.

CONTAINERS

When it comes to containers, the sky's the limit. To start with, most people make do with fairly conventional vases, but as time goes by and they find their feet they tend to acquire special vases that are almost works of art in themselves. If you feel so disposed, there is nothing to stop you making your own – evening classes in pottery are probably the most economical way. Alternatively, artists' suppliers stock materials that are used in the same way as clay, and produce a similar finished result, but don't need to be fired in a kiln. Either way, be prepared to devote a lot of room to your finds, because the urge to collect can become compulsive!

FLOWERS AND FOLIAGE

What sort of things make good subjects for abstract flower arranging? In theory, of course, almost anything could be used. But the things that look best are those that are particularly striking for some reason, be it shape, size or colour. This is because you use a lot less flowers or foliage in the abstract style, so that what you do use really has to make its mark.

A lot of the more exotic, and necessarily expensive, florists' flowers make super subjects for abstract arrangements: proteas, bird of paradise flowers, orchids or spider chrysanthemums, for instance. But plenty of plants which you could perfectly well grow in your own garden will fit the bill just as well, such as paeonies, arum lilies, rhododendrons, garden lilies, roses, daffodils and tulips. Particularly useful are varieties of garden flowers that come in out-of-the-ordinary colours, such as green chrysanthemums and brown roses, or in unusual or striking shapes like the crown imperial lily, parrot tulips or the flowers of dutchman's pipe (*Aristolochia*).

Again, when it comes to foliage, the more striking the shapes the better. Phormium, a relatively new plant to the British has leaves pointed like swords and comes in shades of purple, bronze and green. The castor oil plant, *Fatsia japonica*, has large, leathery, figlike leaves. Consider also bamboos of all kinds, and Trachycarpus, a palm hardy in the southwest of England.

Indoor plants provide good pickings for abstract flower arrangers, too. Try leaves of *Monstera deliciosa*, the breadfruit or Swiss cheese plant; aspidistra; and trailing asparagus fern. Sometimes whole plants can be built into an arrangement; Bromeliads, the so-called urn plants, and their cousins the air plants, which don't have any roots at all, are perfectly at home perched up in bits of dead wood and have just the wierd shapes you want for abstract work. And, unlike most plants, they don't have to stand in a window – they prefer shade.

As well as fresh flowers and foliage, a great deal of preserved material is used in abstract arranging. Much of it consists of things at which the traditional preserved flower arranger would raise an eyebrow. One of the great virtues of abstract flower arranging, that makes it completely different from any other style, is that the way in which the material – flowers, foliage or whatever – is used does not have to resemble the way in which it grows naturally. You see clipped or split leaves; bent or artificially twisted stems; dried material sprayed in the most gaudy colours imaginable; stripped twigs placed horizontally, or even upside down. You'll see stems deliberately crossing each other, or spiralling round flowers; and two-tier arrangements balanced in pieces of wood or even on living plants. In short, all the rules of flower arranging that you ever knew are shattered. But in this style you can get away with it.

An attractive piece of gnarled wood like this provides a good sculptured shape which can be used in many different ways in abstract arrangements. Here it is lying on a pottery dish, with anthurium leaves and a single gerbera. *Arranged by Pamela South*

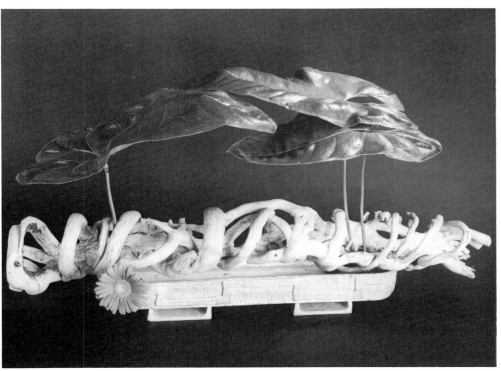

5   Preserved Flowers

Flower arranging isn't a particularly new idea. In England, it started, after a fashion, back in medieval times. The Japanese were doing it way back in the sixth century. And the Chinese took it up it even earlier than that. The Greeks and Romans went in for floral wreaths, worn on the heads of heroes. But they are all relative newcomers to the art compared to the ancient Egyptians, who were arranging flowers over four thousand years ago. And although they are best known for preserving mummies, what the ancient Egyptians can't have kown at the time is that they had accidentially stumbled on the secret of perfect flower preservation.

Of course, they didn't actually need to preserve flowers; their climate was so warm that fresh flowers grew perfectly well all year round. But their 'discovery' of flower preservation all stems from their obsession with the afterlife. They spent much of their lifetime preparing for it. All their important people were buried in gigantic tombs along with all the objects they were going to need in the next world – furniture, chariots, household items and all the rest. From the wall paintings and personal possessions that have been discovered by archaeologists, it's obvious that flowers played an important part in ancient Egyptian life. They were used at all sorts of ceremonial occasions, in processions, and on the tables at banquets, for which huge, multi-tiered arrangements were made. Vases of different sorts were found, including some with multiple spouts which bear a striking similarity to seventeenth-century Delft tulip vases. An egyptologist had to know his vases if he was to avoid some unpleasant surprises – some, known as canopic jars, in sets of four with faces painted on them, would have held not flowers, but mummies' innards. We would have no trouble today recognizing a good many of the flowers used in ancient Egyptian arrangements – marigolds and cornflowers, for instance. They also used sprays of foliage, most of which was taken from their fruit trees – peaches, olives and avocado pear, for instance.

However, some of the things they used are not particularly
well known to us. Water flowers and plants figured very
prominently, because in those days Egypt was little more than
a narrow strip of land running along each bank of the river
Nile, and surrounded by desert. Papyrus, which looks very
much like the umbrella plant we know today as a house plant,
grew in the shallow water at the river's edge. When the
Egyptians weren't using it for flower arranging, they made
paper out of it. But the flower they prized most highly of all
was the lotus. There were two kinds: one was a water lily with
blue flowers, and the other was a tall, bankside plant with
pinky white flowers and leaves like shiny blue saucers on
stalks.

To the ancient Egyptians the lotus was sacred, symbolizing
the perfect flower arising from the mud. Being sacred, it was a
natural candidate for offerings to the gods, particularly those
ones concerned with the elaborate funeral rites designed to
ensure the safe passage of the dead on their journey through to
the afterlife. Any number of wall paintings exist showing piles
of lotus flower offerings being made to the gods. The deceased
and his family would be shown, in scenes taken from his life,
holding or sniffing at lotus flowers. Lotus would also feature
on the stone memorial tablets left outside the tomb to remind
passers-by of his existence.

Fresh flowers would have been used in the funeral
ceremony itelf, and were often left behind in the tomb.
Tutenkhamun's tomb, for instance, contained floral necklaces
which had been worn by guests at his funeral banquet, as well
as flower garlands round the neck of the mummy itself.
Sometimes flowers were placed inside the sarcophagus – the
mummy case – as well. And thousands of years later,
egyptologists may have been a little taken aback to find, along
with all the wonderful treasures, flowers – in a perfect state of
preservation. At one famous burial, the preservation process
worked right down to the scent – when the tomb was opened,
a strong scent of delphinium came out, from a small bunch of
them which had been left inside it several thousand years
earlier. How did they do it?

The answer is that they didn't. It happened all by itself, an
accident of nature. The secret lay in the perfectly dry air sealed
inside the tombs under the desert sand. And that is the basis of
the way in which flowers have been preserved in less
amenable climates ever since.

Coming back to modern-day Europe, with its cold winters
and unpredictable summers, of course we can't get fresh
flowers all year from our gardens as the ancient Egyptians did.
There are times when, if you want them, you just have to buy
them. And if the price is more than you are prepared to pay,
the chances are that you either make do with a few, or go
without. That poses problems for the English, since our
traditional style of flower arranging relies on having lots of

An extremely decorative plaque made from helichrysum, French marigolds and hellebore with beech leaves and cupressus foliage. Spiky quaking grass introduces a contrast of form and helps define the outline of the design, made entirely from dried materials.
Arranged by Maureen Foster

flowers – unless, of course, you find some way of preserving the glut of fresh summer garden flowers to use in winter.

It's not just the British who have these difficulties. The further north you go, the worse the problem becomes, as the climate deteriorates further. In Scandanavia, fresh flowers are so expensive that preserved kinds simply have to be used, far more even than we do.

Since most methods of preservation rely on removing the water from flowers, the damp air of the British Isles doesn't make straightforward drying the answer in all cases, though it can be used for some kinds of flowers. Back in the seventeenth century, the Italians used to dry flowers very successfully in boxes of sand. Since they have a somewhat warmer, drier climate than ours, it seems to have worked pretty well. It is possible to dry flowers in this way now, but in our climate it isn't always very successful, because they tend to take up water from the moisture in the air and gradually go off.

Over the years all sorts of weird and wonderful ways of preserving flowers have been dreamed up. The Victorians were so crazy about flowers that they tried all the means at their disposal in an attempt to preserve them. They made arrangements of dried flowers and ferns and kept them under glass domes. Very often these would just have been air-dried, probably hanging in bunches upside down as we do with everlasting flowers today. But some flowers, especially the larger ones such as roses, would have been dried using the sealing wax method. The ends of the stems were dipped in warm sealing wax, and the flowers arranged while they were still fresh. Then they would have been placed under a glass dome to dry. (In case you were wondering why we don't still do it this way nowadays, it's because it doesn't work very well).

Pressing flowers to make pictures was yet another way of preserving them, once again by removing their natural moisure. Flowers with flat 'faces', such as pansies, were good subjects for this sort of treatment, as they wouldn't be squashed out of shape by the process. Ferns, always favourites with the Victorians, were also much pressed. But some of their pressed pictures were actually made, not of flowers, but of seaweed. In the absence of modern adhesives they stuck them on with milk. It seems to have worked very well, though it might have become a little offensive in warm weather. Most original Victorian dried flower pictures are now badly faded, unfortunately, but suddenly they have come back into fashion, like a good many other Victorian things, and now many modern ones in the Victorian style can be found in the shops.

Besides drying, the Victorians made 'phantom bouquets' from skeletonized leaves. Strong caustic solutions, which must have been rather rough on the hands in the days before rubber gloves, were used to remove the flesh from the leaf 'ribs'. Nowadays you can achieve the same effect by soaking leaves in a solution of bleach for a few days.

One Victorian flower author also reckoned you could preserve flowers by smoking them. But, unlike kippers, flowers were supposed to be smoked over brimstone in a special dual-compartment gadget. The idea was that the flowers were put into one compartment and brimstone in the other. The smoker would be sealed to make it airtight, once the brimstone had been lit. After twenty-four hours the flowers would be taken out, when, according to the writer, they would be completely white. But after hanging in the fresh air for a few hours they would recover their colour, and be ready to use. All very well in theory, but since nobody else ever wrote about the method, or appears to have seen or heard of a brimstone flower smoker, it seems unlikely to have been in common use – if it actually worked at all.

Fortunately, nowadays we have at our disposal much more reliable methods of preserving flowers. Enthusiasts have done a great deal of work to find out just which methods suit which particular flowers. Using chemicals that the Victorians never knew about, it is now possible to preserve most flowers in perfect condition. You can do it yourself at home, without needing all sorts of paraphernalia. Some people have even been known to preserve difficult subjects such as daffodils, given sufficient reason to try. One dedicated preserver is the lady responsible for providing flower arrangements at a certain museum; and, not having the time to keep changing flowers, water or both, she taught herself how to preserve everything she needed to make arrangements to suit the season. So far, visitors have not noticed the difference.

Preserving flowers and foliage*

How many times have you wished that you could keep a special flower, maybe the first rose of summer or flowers from an anniversary bouquet. By following the simple methods of preserving set out below it is possible to keep not only these but many other flowers. There is also a method for preserving foliage to arrange with your preserved flowers, or to arrange with a bunch of fresh flowers from the florist. This is particularly useful in the winter when foliage in the garden is scarce.

PRESERVING FLOWERS

Because of their heads of closely packed minute florets, a few garden flowers fall successfully into the category of 'hang up to dry'. I can recommend yarrow (Achillea filipendulina, Coronation Gold and Cloth of Gold; and Achillea millefolium, Fire King and Cerise Queen) as being particularly suited to this method of preserving known as the Air Method. The following will also produce satisfactory results: globe thistle (*Echinops*) which should be picked before they are fully open; gypsophila; heather (*Erica*), and sea holly (*Eryngium*). Strawflowers (*Helichrysum*) and other so-called annual everlasting flowers such as statice (*Limonium*) should also be preserved in this way. The stem of strawflowers have a habit of becoming limp just below the flower head as they dry out. If these are to be used in an arrangement it would be advisable to replace the stems with wires as explained on page 92. The ideal conditions for hanging these flowers to dry are cool, dry, airy and dark.

To obtain successful results when preserving other garden flowers will require the use of a desiccant. Special flower-preserving crystals provide a simple, safe and effective desiccant which is formulated to remove the natural moisture yet retain the structure, contours and colour of many flowers which would otherwise be destroyed if they were just hung up to dry. These crystals can be reactivated after use, enabling

* This section has kindly been contributed by Maureen Foster.

them to be used over and over again indefinately. (Details for purchase are given at the end of this book).

With the exception of dark red flowers with a blue undertone (which tend to darken) the quality of most other colours remains true when treated by this process. Ideally, first experiments should be carried out with easy-to-handle flower shapes such as daisies, before progressing to trumpet-shaped flowers such as hollyhocks, or the more intricate petal formation of a rose. It is necessary in the process to use airtight containers, preferably tins, although plastic containers will do quite well. The size of container will be related to the size and quantity of flowers being preserved in each batch; the fewer the better should be the beginners' motto.

PREPARATION FOR PRESERVING

Have the container and crystals ready before gathering your flowers, which should be picked when quite dry. Mid-day in high summer is a time to be avoided as the intense heat will cause the flowers to become limp and therefore difficult to handle and process successfully. A thorough inspection of each flower is essential – damaged petals and insect holes can mar the beauty of a preserved flower, while flowers that are past maturity will tend to shatter when preserved.

WIRING

It will be necessary at this stage to check carefully the stem of each type of flower. If the flower is firm and woody-textured, such as delphinium, it will preserve successfully, but if it is fleshy – as is a dahlia – the stem will have to be replaced by a wire before preserving (florists' wire can be used for this). Using only a short length of wire, push one end through the centre of the flower; allow the other end to become embedded in the centre. During the preserving process the sap will cause the wire to corrode slightly and ensure a firm bond between flower and wire. This operation cannot be successfully carried out after the flower is preserved, but the wire can of course be lengthened later simply by wiring it onto a second wire.

THE BASIC PRESERVING PROCESS

Spoon a layer of crystals into the tin to a depth of about ½ inch (12.5 mm) and position the flowers according to their shape – for example, daisies need to be placed in the 'faces down, stalks up' position, but a single hollyhock bloom should be laid on its side. The secret of the success of this process lies in covering the flowers. Do not spoon the crystals over the top, but around each flower, letting them fall naturally between the petals – except for trumpet shapes such as the hollyhock which must first be filled with crystals before covering, to prevent flattening. It cannot be over-emphasised that the careful way in which the flowers are covered is the essence of success in preserving flowers. The length of time required for each batch of flowers to preserve will vary from, for example, two days for lawn daisies to fourteen days for an African marigold, depending on the texture and thickness of the petals and the density of each flower.

The following flowers are particularly suitable for desiccant preserving, but the enthusiastic reader will soon relate the texture and form of these to other similar species and so discover how interesting and absorbing this aspect of flower arranging can be.

Anemone
Camomile (Anthemis)
Dahlia: decorative and pom pom varieties, not cactus
Delphinium
Freesia
Fuchsia: wire individual florets for miniature arrangements
Golden Rod (Solidago): can be preserved by the air method but results are not particularly good
Lilac
Roses: concentrate on partly-opened small roses
Zinnia

The conditions under which preserved flowers are displayed and stored are of particular importance – a warm dry room is ideal. The atmosphere of unheated rooms can contain moisture which preserved flowers will quickly re-absorb. Due to the petal formation of some flowers this can cause petals to flop, but many flowers will be unaffected. While flowers are not in use they should be stood in a block of dry oasis and enclosed in an airtight tin which contains a small quantity of dry preserving crystals.

Foliage for use with preserved flowers can be preserved in a desiccant but, while it is an ideal process for autumn-coloured foliages, evergreen and summer gathered deciduous foliages remain more pliable and therefore easier to handle if preserved by standing them in a mixture of one part glycerine and water together. Split the ends of the stems before standing them in the mixture. For successful results the container should be stood in a warm place to ensure a more rapid intake of the mixture. The preserving time will vary from four days to between four and five weeks, depending on the texture of the foliage. As the leaves drink up this mixture, most foliage will change colour but the results will give a pleasing contrast to preserved flowers or, as I have already mentioned, as a background for a few fresh flowers. However, if using them in this way it would be advisable to varnish the ends of the stems or seal them in some other way to prevent mould forming as they stand in water.

---

* This section has kindly been contributed by Maureen Foster.

In the space available it has been possible for me to do little more than introduce the reader to the subject of preserving by showing how easy it is to preserve a wide variety of flowers and foliage and make up a simple plaque (see instructions and step-by-step drawings on pages 102–105). Enthusiasm, imagination and an awareness of colour, shape and form are the only requirements needed to launch the beginner into an exciting, fascinating and inexpensive hobby. The creative uses, not only of preserved flower and foliage but of many other natural plant materials, are endless.

STORING AND LOOKING AFTER PRESERVED FLOWERS

Once you have started to amass a collection of preserved flowers, the big problem is what to do with them all. Only a certain amount in arrangements will be needed at any one time – you'll want to ring the changes a little, and not just keep the same ones on display for ever and a day.

Since the flowers are so brittle, storage can become a bit of a problem. The safest way to keep bunches of everlasting flowers, grasses and other long-stemmed subjects which have been air-dried is in bunches, hanging upside down somewhere out of the way. A cupboard under the stairs or in a spare bedroom is fine; garages and sheds are not very suitable as they tend to be damp, and for good storage dry air is essential. More precious flowers, such as water lilies and other subjects that have been dried with the aid of a chemical such as silica, need more careful storage. They are best kept until needed in airtight biscuit tins, or plastic containers like the kind ice cream comes in, along with a small quantity of silica crystals to ensure that they keep perfectly dry. Once you take preserved flowers out of store to use them, it helps if they are again kept in as dry an environment as possible. Modern central heating usually means that the air indoors keeps very dry anyway, but halls, cloakrooms and so on are sometimes damp, which means that the flowers may eventually mildew. However, the biggest problem with preserved flowers is dust. To avoid disturbing an arrangement, dust may be gently blown off, or you can use a hairdrier on the cold setting. It also pays to keep preserved flowers as far as possible out of bright direct sunlight, which tends to fade them. But at the end of the day, although preserved flowers last very much longer than fresh ones, they do eventually lose their looks and need replacing.

Growing your own flowers for preserving

If you have a garden, even if it is only a small one, it is possible to grow your own ready-preserved flowers. You may even find there are plenty already growing there that can be harvested for preserving. Not all flowers are good subjects, so unless you are experienced it is best to start with something easy.

The following are a selection that are not only suitable for the beginner to preserve, but are also not difficult to grow.

EVERLASTING FLOWERS

Helichrysum, statice, clary, acanthus, gypsophila and achillea can be grown from seed, but plants are often available in garden centres in spring.

OTHER GOOD PRESERVING FLOWERS

Ornamental onion (Allium species), artichoke, astilbe, mollucella (bells of Ireland), cornflower, feverfew; bulbs of Allium species can be bought from garden centres in autumn, and artichoke and astilbe plants are usually available in spring; the rest can be grown from seed.

GARDEN SHRUBS

Hydrangea, including lacecaps; roses; and *Garrya elliptica* for catkins. Plants are available from most garden centres.

PLANTS FOR FOLIAGE TO PRESERVE

Hardy ferns, *Stachys lanata* (rabbits' ears) with its hairy silver leaves, ivy, eucalyptus, beech including copper and purple varieties, hosta, *Fatsia japonica* (castor oil plant); again, plants are readily available from nurseries and garden centres.

SEEDPODS, SEEDHEADS

Physalis (Chinese lanterns), eryngium (sea holly), *Echinops ritro* (globe thistle), nigella (love-in-a-mist), honesty, teasel, poppy; all can be grown from seed.

GOURDS

Ornamental gourds can easily be grown in the garden rather like marrows, from seed sown in spring. The selection available includes Turk's Turban, a bright orange variety with green and red stripes; bottle gourds, which can also be used as containers for dried flowers; and mixtures of small, multicoloured and variously shaped gourds. All must be left on the vine until the autumn to ripen, then brought indoors to dry out thoroughly before being arranged. They can be varnished before use, and will keep for years.

GRASSES

Animated oats (*Avena sterilis*) and Quaking grass (*Briza maxima*) are two of the best-known ornamental grasses that can be dried for flower arranging, though there are plenty of others offered through the seed catalogues. Most are annuals, sown in spring and picked in summer when the heads are fully formed. If you leave them to dry on the plants you risk having them drop their seed all over the place. After drying the head upside down in a shed you can 'set' them with hairspray – but treat with care as this makes them even more highly inflammable than normal.

WILD FLOWERS

Many, especially heartsease, toadflax, for instance, make ideal subjects for pressing. A number of species are now protected plants and cannot be picked, but since seed is available either of single varieties or of mixtures, wild flowers can easily be grown at home and are a lovely way to transform a rough patch of woodland, hedge bottom or ditch side. Treat wild flowers as hardy annuals, scattering seed in prepared ground during spring where you want them to flower.

OTHER MISCELLANEOUS 'PROPS'

Try contorted willow (*Salix matsudana tortuosa*) for extravagantly twisted stems, and its relative *Salix sachalinensis setsuka*, which has fasciated stems making strange flattened growths. For cones grow *Abies koreana*, one of the few ornamental conifers that will produce cones while plants are still small; its cones are a most attractive blue-mauve colour.

Containers for preserved flowers

Since they don't need to hold water, you have a much more exciting choice of containers for preserved flowers than you do if you limit yourself to working with fresh material that must have its feet in water. With preserved material, the container can actually be considered more as a base to the arrangement than as a holder.

Given a little imagination, you can find all sorts of most attractive preserved flower holders among everyday items – junk shops are a great source of damaged or broken objects that can be converted into unusual holders for flowers that don't need water. Ornaments, old glass domes, fancy wooden or mother of pearl boxes with the lid propped open – all can be used for preserved flowers.

Alternatively, you could make your own containers from otherwise unwanted household or even natural materials. Driftwood makes one of the nicest 'containers' for preserved flowers. You can find your own out in the countryside and

Preserved flowers
arranged in a silver
candelabra for a
special occasion. The
flowers are chosen to
harmonize with the
candle, which is blue

often even in your own garden. Old hawthorn stumps and roots and old ivy stems from tree trunks both make especially good 'driftwood'. The best place to find good pieces is where a farmer is grubbing out an old hedge, but do ask before taking anything, and avoid trespassing to make your 'finds'. Sometimes it is possible to find genuine driftwood on the beach, if you know of a spot where the current tends to bring things ashore.

Hunting for driftwood certainly enlivens a country ramble, but the fun really starts when you bring it home. Most pieces will need a bit of attention before they are fit to use. First step in the preparation process is to clean it up. A good scrub in warm soapy water may do for some of the not too bad pieces. Otherwise a twenty-four-hour soak in a tub of strongish bleach solution is the answer. This will get rid of lurking creepy-crawlies that often hide in inaccessible spots, and which make such unwelcome guests in the living room. After using bleach, rinse the wood a couple of times in clean water before leaving it to dry.

Some driftwood has most attractive bark, which is a feature worth leaving. Other pieces, however, are less well endowed and look better if stripped of bark. Old bark is often loose and can easily be picked away with pliers; the bark from green wood will not come away easily and is better left; alternatively the piece can be left out in the garden for a year or so to dry out and let nature take its course. Once you have got a piece of driftwood stripped of its bark, you don't have to leave it like that. If you wish, you can colour or shine it. Colouring can be used either to enhance its natural colour, or to jazz it up with a completely false one. Ordinary woodworking stains are suitable, as are colour-tinted varnishes; all are available from DIY stores. You could even use different coloured shoe waxes, which is probably the best way of applying an instant natural look.

Victorian-style pressed flower pictures

Now that they are back in vogue, it is good fun to try your hand at making your own. You can use the same technique to make personalized birthday and valentine cards, just as the Victorians did. And when the children want something to do in the holidays, this is something they can have a got at too. It isn't difficult, and thanks to modern adhesives and fixatives the results are generally better than the Victorians would have had.

The best sorts of flowers to press, as mentioned earlier, are those that have naturally flat profiles – flowers with faces, such as pansies, are best: heartsease and violets, including the Victorian favourite parma violets, if you can get them, are all excellent. Flowers to avoid are those with thick, fleshy petals, or cup- and trumpet-shaped blooms which just squash out of shape when you press them. For foliage, ferns press well and make interesting shapes in a design, especially the ones with smaller leaves, such as maidenhair fern, which is grown as a pot plant. You can even try your hand with seaweed. But just by looking around your own garden you'll probably be able to find all sorts of other leaves and flowers to press – even weeds often provide useful material.

Make sure the flowers are dry when you collect them. Pick only perfect specimens – any flaws look glaringly obvious when you try to make up your picture.

As for equipment, the Victorian flower presser would most likely have had a proper flower press, which looks rather like a solid version of a tennis racket press – a pair of small boards

A collage made entirely from natural plant material that has been preserved – grasses, the bracts of wild knapweed, scales taken from monkey puzzle and fir cones, and tiny silver senecio leaves. The owl's eyes are made from preserved leaves which have been trimmed to the exact size and shape required

sandwiched together, with thumbscrews in the corners to tighten them together. If you want to do the thing properly, you can still get flower presses at some handicraft shops, and at the time of writing Laura Ashley sell them. Otherwise you can do perfectly well using a set of encyclopedias – on a good firm base to ensure even pressure – to provide the necessary weight.

Whichever form of pressure you use, you need to lay your flowers between two sheets of clean white blotting paper. This is essential, as you must have something to absorb the moisture that is pressed out of the flowers – pressing is really just another means of preserving flowers by drying them.

Lay the flowers out on the blotting paper in such a way that don't touch each other. Make sure the petals are all laid out straight, not crossing over or otherwise out of place, because that is how they will look – permanently – after they come out of the press. Next, put the second sheet of blotting paper over the top, and tighten the thumbscrews or pile on the encyclopedias.

It is difficult to say exactly how long it takes to press flowers. It depends a lot on the temperature and humidity at the time, and it varies between different kinds of flowers. The only safe way to tell is to open up periodically and have a look. When they are ready they will be completely stiff and will lift easily off the blotting paper without sticking. If you take them out too soon, before they are properly dried, they will go off quickly. And if you leave them too long, the colours will have faded. By the time you have done a few experience with tell you when they are just right.

The next thing to do is to make up a design. You can lay out the flowers and leaves and move them round a bit while you see how they look best, but they are terribly fragile and too much handling is rather risky. Alternatively, you could rough out a few ideas in pencil first, then just make up the finished design in flowers. A square of thick art paper, hessian or velvet makes a good background for a pressed flower picture; for do-it-yourself cards, use good-quality writing – the thicker the better – folded in two. As a change from plain white or grey, try using pastel colours, perhaps choosing one which picks out one of the colours from the flowers.

As for fixing them in place, use one of the special adhesives sold for handicrafts. The next problem to tackle is how to stop the flowers from fading. The Victorian lady, without the benefit of modern handicraft aids, had to touch up her pictures with watercolour paint; that and a coat of varnish over the top afterwards was about the best she could do. Nowadays, once the adhesive has dried you can spray a completed flower picture with an aerosol fixative, again of the type sold for handicrafts. This covers the flowers with a sort of invisible film, sealing the flower in and the damp out, so the colour lasts better.

For the finishing touch, you could mount the whole thing in a frame. Brand-new frames are available in gift shops and some stores as well as from artists' suppliers and photography shops – but they may be expensive. Good secondhand frames with an authentic antique character can still be found at a reasonable price by hunting in junks shops.

Seed collages

A completely different kind of plant picture can be made up from seeds. Seed collages, as they are called, are quicker to do than pressed flower pictures as you don't have to do any preparation. Just shop around for some brightly coloured or interestingly shaped seeds, design a picture or pattern, and fill it in using seeds stuck to the same kinds of backing material that you would use for pressed flower pictures. You could make a completely abstract pattern, designed to show off the very different nature of the different kinds of seeds – this is the

A collage with three designs made from wild grasses, shown to advantage against a black background. The top and bottom designs also contain glycerined molucella leaves for added interest

way I think they work best. Alternatively you could go for a realistic picture of a plant, bird or landscape, for instance, just using different seeds to fill in the different coloured areas.

Suitable seeds will often be found in pet shops and health food stores – where you can see what you are getting – as well as in packets from garden centres, where you need to know what to expect.

For a selection of seeds to give a good range of colours, shapes and textures try sunflower, sycamore, parsnip (round, flat seeds), millet, lentils (red, green and brown), ricinus (castor oil plant, which has multicoloured seeds looking like exotic beetles), buckwheat (pyramid-shaped seeds), split green and yellow peas, honesty, and conifer seeds shaken from their cones.

You could even combine seeds with other sorts of collage materials, such as bits of scrunched up magazine, feathers or shells, to make a really exotic creation.

Step by step instructions for making a simple plaque*

Bases for plaques are easily made from stiff, non-pliable cardboard. Coloured mounting board, obtainable from art shops, can be used but ordinary plain cardboard covered with a remnant of fabric makes a more attractive base. I prefer to use round or oval shapes for plaques, since they avoid the hard, pointed corners of the square and oblong shapes. Round shapes of any size are easily drawn using a pair of compasses, or alternatively a suitable plate or saucer.

It may prove slightly more difficult to draw an oval, but look around the house for a picture frame, meat plate or table mat; there are in fact many things which can be used as a template from which to cut a perfect oval. The size can easily be enlarged or reduced simply by measuring and redrawing the line before cutting with sharp scissors or a craft knife.

1. Cut a piece of fabric ¾ inch larger all round than the cardboard shape, making quite sure that you cut this on the straight of the fabric grain.

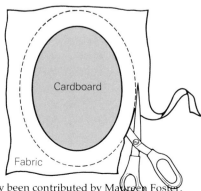

Cardboard

Fabric

* This section has kindly been contributed by Maureen Foster.

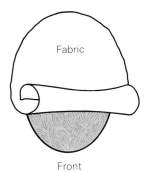

Fabric

Front

2. Cover one side of the cardboard with a thin coat of latex adhesive. Lay the fabric over the latexed surface, smoothing it as you work but being careful not to stretch it.

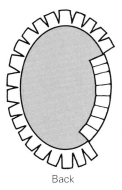

Back

3. Turn the base over and cut V-shaped notches in the edge of the fabric; this will enable it to lie evenly. To ensure a neat, smooth edge to the finished base avoid cutting these right up to the edge of the cardboard. Spread a thin band of adhesive round the edge of the cardboard and turn the notched edge over on to the adhesive and smooth it down.

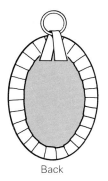

Back

4. To provide a means of hanging your plaque use either a special sticky hanging tab (available from most art shops) or a curtain ring attached by a small piece of tape which should be firmly stuck to the back of the base.

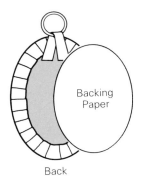

Back

5. Cut a piece of paper slightly smaller than the size of your base and stick this over the back to cover the raw edges and produce a neat finish.

6. The plaque base is now ready for you to prepare your arrangement. The design I have chosen to use clearly illustrates the necessary graduation of plant materials which is all-important in the making of a plaque. You may find it helpful to draw a few guide-lines with chalk but I prefer to arrange my plant materials directly on to the base and then to keep moving them about until I have created a pleasing design.

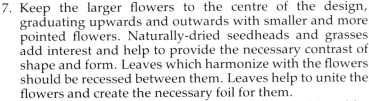

7. Keep the larger flowers to the centre of the design, graduating upwards and outwards with smaller and more pointed flowers. Naturally-dried seedheads and grasses add interest and help to provide the necessary contrast of shape and form. Leaves which harmonize with the flowers should be recessed between them. Leaves help to unite the flowers and create the necessary foil for them.

A more pleasing and professional effect is achieved by sticking your flowers slightly on their side rather than faces up. Use a quick drying contact adhesive such as UHU and always apply it to the plant material and not to the base.

8. A matching cord stuck to the edge of the base gives a decorative edge to the finished plaque and helps to create the appearance of a frame.

6 A Florist's Eye View of Flowers

What do the Miss World competition, the captain's cocktail party on the *QE2*, the Horse of the Year Show and Mrs Thatcher's desk all have in common?

The answer is flowers. At just about any event you care to name you'll find flowers. The rich and famous love to be surrounded by them. Flowers are the universal window dressing that gives the finishing touch, be it motor show or horse show, society luncheon or press conference. You'll find flowers at any occasion, large or small, wherever somebody wants to make the occasion.

How do they get there? It's all done by florists of course. Very often even quite small shops like the one in your local high street will be involved in surprisingly high-powered contract work that you'd never know anything about if you just called in for a bunch of daffs. A florist might be designing displays of orchids from Singapore for the International Garden Festival one day, and making up a bouquet for your auntie's birthday the next.

But if you think it sounds like being a sophisticated or even an easy job, take a look at what goes on behind the window dressing! To most people, the only difference between a florist and a flower arranger is that the one gets paid to arrange flowers, whilst the other does it for nothing. But there's a lot more to floristry than simple arranging flowers. So exactly what is the difference?

The answer all stems from two thorny old chestnuts, time and money. When it comes to the question of time, the florist can't afford to be a flower arranger – she has a list full of orders to complete to a punishingly tight schedule. On average, she'll have less than ten minutes to make up an arrangement over which a flower arranger at home could quite happily spend half the afternoon. In a day, the chances are that the florist will probably have made up more arrangements than the average flower arranger would do in a month.

As for the question of cost, the florist has to work with whatever flowers are available in the shop at the time – and keep a constant tally of the cost so it fits the price set by the customer. Any mistakes, and the shop will be out of pocket at the end of the day. But the flower arranger working on an arrangement at home doesn't count the cost, or the value of her time. And if she's doing the flowers for a special occasion, the chances are she'll splash out on something special – like out-of-season roses, or carnations – instead of just relying on whatever happens to be in the garden.

The glamorous image

But what about the glamour side – the exotic locations, famous celebrities and all the trimmings? Well, I'm sorry to say that even the most glamorous-sounding jobs are not always quite so enviable when you are the person actually doing them. Fancy being the florist on the *QE2* during one of their round-the-world cruises?

Being ship's florist sounds like lots of fun, but unfortunately it's no good applying for the job if you are expecting it to be a constant round of swimming, sunning, cocktail parties and visits ashore; there's too much work to do for that. In fact, a sea-going florist's feet hardly have time to touch the ground. First of all there are the corsages to be made – each lady passenger receives one when she joins the ship; she will also find a flower arrangement in her cabin to help make her feel at home. And since most people join the cruise for a few weeks at a time rather than doing the complete tour, that's already quite a lot of flowers to do. Then there are arrangements for the ship's public rooms – all the restaurants have flowers on the tables, as well as some in the lounges. Not to mention the ship's potted plants – hundreds of them – which have to be tended.

One of the more unusual duties of the *QE2*'s floating florist is to set out a row of potted palms along the red-carpeted gangplank every time the ship docks to pick up passengers. And, of course, she has to collect them up again afterwards. Then there is the shipboard florist's shop to run; it caters for guests who want flowers for birthday bouquets, or for their own cocktail parties, some of which can be pretty elaborate occasions. Long hours are very much the order of the day. As well as the actual flower arranging, the ship's florist has to order all her own flowers; and, to be sure that they are ready and waiting when the ship docks, they have to be ordered two weeks ahead of time.

Far from seeing the world at someone else's expense, the florist will be lucky to leave the ship at all, particularly at embarkation ports when there are new arrivals to make arrangements for. Are there any perks to the job? There's always the romance of the sea air, of course – one floating florist tells me she's had more proposals of marriage on board than she can remember.

The story isn't much different for all those so-called glamour jobs doing flowers for horse shows, society parties and the like. On the face of it, it seems like a super-pleasant way of earning your crust. And up to a point it is. But behind the façade there's lots of hard and often heavy work, with inevitable long hours and late-night finishes.

The daily grind

That's one side of the florist's work, and one that lots of high street florists find themselves involved in from time to time, let alone the top-class West End variety who often specialize in the more glamorous aspects. But what about the everyday side of a florist's business, running the shop? A normal day's work for most florist's shop runs to a preset pattern. The mornings are taken up with making up the day's orders, which will probably be written on a board to make certain that nothing gets forgotten. The shop will most likely run their own van, and delivering arrangements and bouquets will employ someone's time for much of the day, even at not-so-busy times of the year. And now that telephone flower services such as Interflora are so widespread, with customers able to pick up the telephone and order flowers to be sent just about anywhere in the world, the corner florist may be given orders for local delivery from just about anywhere.

The other big job for the morning is receiving the new consignments of flowers coming into the shop and conditioning them. A florist's idea of conditioning involves much more than we do at home. This is because the florist normally gets her flowers from the wholesale markets, and there is a good chance they will have been in transit for several days between the time they were cut and when she receives them. To make sure that they last as long as they should, she must not only cut off the bottom of their stems as we would at home, but give them other specific treatments as well. The precise recipe for conditioning varies with different kinds of flowers, and it is part of the florist's job to know how best to care for all the various types she has to deal with.

In the afternoon, there might still be orders to make up at specially busy times of year. Otherwise it is a good time for getting ahead with other jobs that can be prepared in advance, like wiring moss to preshaped frames for the special bases that some types of arrangement require, or making up arrangements of silk flowers.

Of course, all this behind-the scenes activity takes place out at the back in the workroom, the nerve centre of the business. Here you'll find the florist's stock-in-trade – collections of wires of all sizes, blocks of flower arranging foam, cellophane sleeves for bouquets, ribbons and bows for the finishing touches, and of course buckets of flowers constantly being

Top left Picking gerbera in a Dutch nursery. *Top right*, a special gadget
guillotines all the stems to an even length, ready for their final
packing, *above*, and they are then ready to be sent to the market

dipped into. For much of the time the workroom doesn't look terribly tidy. There just isn't time to clear up until the end of the day's work. So piles of discarded leaf trimmings and bits of stems lie about all over the place. The work proceeds at an almost unbelievable pace, yet the casual visitor calling in at the shop would never imagine what a hive of activity there was just off-stage.

Special occasions

Knowing what a normal day is like, it's difficult to imagine how florists could possibly pull out any extra stops to cope with busy seasons, but amazingly they do. Valentine's Day, Christmas, Easter and Mother's Day are the florists' equivalent of climbing Everest. At these times the girls might work half the night to get special arrangements and bouquets ready. The trouble is that everyone sending flowers wants their order delivered first. It's not surprising, when you think about it, because anyone receiving a bouquet wants to be able to enjoy it for the whole of the special day, not just the last hour or two of it. Solving that problem is one of the florist's bigger headaches; often whole squads of spare-time drivers with estate cars will be co-opted to do the rounds. On days like this you'll find the florists' aunties, granny, son and his schoolfriends alike all out there lending a hand.

But getting the orders out on time isn't the only problem. Many of these special days fall at times when fresh flowers are out of season and therefore rather expensive, which isn't good for either customer or florists. The florists would much prefer Valentine's Day, for instance, to be rescheduled in June, when the favourite Valentine flowers, red roses, are in season. They would be much cheaper than they are on 14 February, and everyone would be happier – the customer because he would get more flowers for his money, and the florist because a happy customer is more likely to come back and buy flowers again if he thinks they are good value for money and not just expensive treats for a special occasion.

Fashions exist in floristry as they do in most other areas, and, now that we are used to the idea of giving flowers for special occasions, it seems we are starting to look for something a little more exciting than the standard bouquet. To cater for the demand, florists have come up with all sorts of novel ideas for incorporating flowers into other gifts. You can, for instance, send a floral greetings card – instead of a picture of flowers on the front, like the sort you get from card shops, the florist's version has a real live flower arrangement peeking out through the front. Of you might prefer the idea of giving a box of chocolates, but again, instead of a picture of flowers on the box, you could order one with real flowers on it. Both ideas are gaining ground rapidly, especially for Mother's Day.

A novel way of
sending flowers: a
blooming Valentine
card

In the USA they have one special occasion that hasn't
reached us yet – Secretaries' Week. Note: it isn't Secretaries'
Day – somewhere, a smart marketing man has worked out that
if one boss gives his secretary a bunch of flowers or a box of
chocs on the Monday, then by the end of the week every
secretary in the place will be up in arms if she hasn't had the
same treatment. It is all a bit underhand by our standards, so it
doesn't seem likely that we'll ever see this particular trend
repeated in Britain, thank goodness.

Quite apart from the designated special days that are marked in all the diaries, there are days that are special to individual people – birthdays, anniversaries and weddings. And although it is possible to make up your own special arrangements for these occasions, going to a florist will give you more time to do those things you can't farm out to an expert. And since the florist is an expert, you can rely on getting work that is well done, and won't let you down by dying or dropping at the last moment. If you can find time to discuss your requirements well beforehand, the florist can probably come up with some new ideas, or get hold of something extra special for you if you want it.

For a wedding, for instance, you could have neckbands, bracelets and hats made of real flowers and petals. You might like real floral decorations for the cake instead of the usual kind. As a change from traditional wedding bouquets you could choose small, rounded Victorian posies encased in a frill – the perfect foil to some of the period-style wedding dresses now in fashion. For a very special party, florists will make up arrangements designed to illustrate a particular theme, or to reflect somebody's special interests. One of the most unusual special orders I have heard of was for a party given by her colleagues in honour of a retiring powder room attendant. They presented her with a life-sized floral loo made of red roses. And that's something you won't find instructions for in the manual of floristry!

How to be a florist

There are plenty of people who dream of running a florist's shop of their very own. As a pipe dream it's a very nice idea, but, as we've seen, the reality is rather different from the romantic image of the job.

The trouble is that anyone can set up as a florist, without any training or even knowing what they are doing. Properly qualified florists running reputable shops are naturally not at all keen on the idea. It's not that they dislike the competition – far from it. Competition raises professional standards, which is good for the business. The trouble with unqualified, 'amateur' florists is that they often turn out second-rate work, or worst of all sell flowers that have not been properly cared for and which don't last, thus debasing the whole trade in the eyes of the disappointed customer, who has no way of knowing a good florist from a bad one until it's too late.

Or can they? There's a lot you can tell from a quick glance round the shop. Qualified florists are more likely to belong to one of the big organizations such as Interflora, whose signs will be on show. The flowers will look fresh, and, most important, when you get them home they will last well in

Dutch florist's

Japanese florist's

water. And if you place an order it will be ready for collection on time.

It's the training that makes all the difference; properly qualified florist's may spend years training not just how to care for, condition and arrange all the different kinds of flowers, but much else too. They learn art and design, horticulture and botany, commercial display techniques, business studies and first aid. And they learn all the tricks of the trade: how to wire flowers, make up buttonholes and a thousand and one other things that the flower arranger at home would never dream of. Day release courses, for trainees who need to earn and learn at the same time, fill in the theory, while the practical side is absorbed by actually doing it back at the shop. Trainees learn the business from the bottom up, starting with the most basic of routine chores under the supervision of fully qualified florists. Alternatively, there are full-time courses, where very intensive instruction gives you a qualification in a much shorter time.

But whichever sort of course a florist takes, she doesn't have to stop learning at all. After she's taken her basic qualification, she can go on to study for the Society of Florists' Diploma, which is when the fun really starts. Florists at this level learn not so much by listening to lectures or by reading textbooks, but by looking at other people's work in exhibitions and competitions. I don't mean the sort of thing that the amateur flower arrange goes to, either, but the floristry world's very own private shows, most of which are never open to the public. Competition classes are quite unlike anything you find on the amateur flower arrangers' circuit; they are more in tune with the world in which the florist works. It isn't so much the finished arrangement that is judged as the florist herself, and how she arrives at her finished result.

Even the classes are different. Whereas the amateur may be asked to interpret a song, film title or famous quotation in flowers, the professional is asked to produce an arrangement for an ambassador's cocktail party, a bouquet for a spring bride, or occasionally fun things like dressing a mannequin in flowers. And while the amateur has as long as she wants to make her arrangement, the professional will usually compete against the clock, simulating the conditions under which she normally has to work. The amateur always has the chance to design and practise her competition arrangements beforehand, and bring her own choice of flowers with her on the day. But the professional has to work with whatever is provided for her – and in one class, the notorious Pandora's box, she won't even be allowed to see her materials until the clock has started and the countdown begun. The sort of things inside Pandora's box would leave your average flower arranger wondering what on earth you could make out of them. Imagine being asked to make an arrangment for a rainy day, using a mixture of flowers, umbrellas and gum boots?

Very rarely can be uninitiated glimpse the secret world of the super-florist in action, but one of the very few events which the public can look in on is Interflora's Florist of the Year Show, which is held in a different town each year. Top florists may go on to travel the world, taking part in international exhibitions and competitions, or perhaps into the rarified heights of judging them.

An entry in a 'Pandora's Box' floristry competition, in which the competitors have to make an arrangement from whatever materials are provided

Creativity is obviously an absolute must for a would-be florist, but artistic ability alone isn't enough. Apart from a good general education, it takes physcial stamina and good health to be a florist – think of all those heavy boxes of flowers to be shifted about, and the occasional but regular bouts of long hours.

The private life of the flower

Despite everything, the florist is actually just the tip of the iceberg in the flower trade – the end link in a whole chain of people who work, often very unsocial hours, so that we can have fresh flowers. Take a look at Covent Garden flower market, at 3.30 am. While the rest of us are still asleep, market salesmen are hard at work bridging the gap between shops who want to buy and growers who want to sell – regardless of whether they are English or foreign.

The flower market looks rather like the sort of street market you find in some town centres on Saturdays, except of course that it is much bigger. Each firm has its own pitch, with its goods on display where customers call to see what's on offer today. Just like a street market, it's a very close community where everybody knows everybody else; they may actually be related to each other – sometimes whole families work together, passing on the business from father to son.

Although the market is made up of so many different traders, there is an extraordinary kind of telepathy at work when it comes to prices. Try as you might, you won't find a lot of difference in price between the same kind of produce on one stand and another. Nobody ever seems to discuss prices with each other, and most certainly nobody ever puts prices up on a board for all to see – but mysteriously, although the prices may rise and fall from one day to the next, everyone asks pretty much the same on every stand.

Knowing this, you might wonder why buyers bother to shop around. The thing is that they don't really. They tend to have their own favourite firms where they get on with the salesman and swap stories and jokes. It's much more like a club where people happen to do business, especially when you compare it to the comparatively aseptic Dutch flower auctions. At Covent Garden, buyers and sellers queue for coffee and bacon butties at one of the roving tea trollies. Then they'll go for breakfast at the close of business – around the time most people are thinking of getting up.

Covent Garden, although the best known of the English markets, is by no means the only one. Most of the big cities will have their own fruit, veg. and flower market where buyers and sellers in the area do business together. But not all the people who sell flowers go to market themselves to buy them. Many larger florists do, to be sure of getting the best available. But many smaller outlets especially rely on the services of a wholesaler who buys a selection of things at the market and sells it door-to-door at small florist's shops, greengrocers, garden centres or farm shops.

Unlike the Dutch system, where growers have to become a member of the auction that sells their produce and send all their output through it, in this country growers are free to sell wherever they please. We don't have much in the way of co-operatives and certainly nothing approaching the scale of the Dutch auction system. Most growers choose to send their produce to the nearest market, just to keep transport costs down. But if a market at the other end of the country is getting a much better price, they are just as likely to send their truckload there instead.

Quite a lot of produce changes hands without ever going near a market, though. Many growers have forged their own links with local shops who buy from them at the farm gate. This way the buyer gets the pick of the crop, and the seller knows how much he has made without waiting to see the returns from the market salesman. The customer benefits too, getting fresher flowers that have gone virtually straight from the ground to the vase.

Compared to growing a few flowers in the garden at home, it is surprising just how much goes into producing a commercial crop of flowers. Take chrysanthemums, for instance. They are one of the most popular of florists' flowers, turned out in their millions by English growers every year; and not just in the autumn, when they grow in the garden anyway – but all year round. Coaxing flowers to bloom out of season is a tricky business at the best of times, but when your whole livelihood depends on it everything has got to be right. Nothing gets left to chance, from the greenhouses themselves right down to the last detail affecting the feeding, watering and heating of the crop. Everything is done automatically. Even the light is rigorously controlled. It has to be, since this is the thing that triggers the plants into thinking that it is autumn, bringing them into flower out of season. In summer the grower will 'black out' his plants with black polythene screens to give them artificially long nights, to bring them into flower. And in winter he'll do the opposite, turning on the lights in the middle of the night to give them two nights with a make-believe day in between.

There is always work to be done with flowers like chrysanthemums. Not long after the cuttings are planted they have to be 'stopped' – taking the tops out of the small plants makes them grow several shoots with a flower on each, instead of just one. Then later, when the first flower buds appear, the grower has to go round again disbudding. If he wants a single large flower at the top of each stem, he'll have to remove the small buds from the cluster to let the crown bud develop. If he wants spray chrysanthemums, with lots of smaller flowers clustered together on a single stem, then he'll nip out the large crown bud at the top of the stem and leave the rest. And when the flowers are barely open, it's time to pick and pack the crop, leaving just enough time to sterilize the soil before the next lot of cuttings need planting. Then the whole cycle starts again.

Of course, that's just the chrysanthemum story – each kind of flower you buy, whether it's lilies, freesias, roses, anemones or anything else, has its own equally exacting production schedule.

Further Information

These organizations and books will help you get your new-found interest in flowers and flower arranging off the ground.

Organizations

National Association of Flower Arrangement Societies of Great Britain (NAFAS), 21 Denbigh Street, London SW1V 2HF
The governing body of flower arrangement societies in Britain. They will put you in touch with a local flower club who hold demonstrations and competitions etc. organized under their auspices, catering for all the various styles of arranging. Members receive a copy of their quarterly magazine, *The Flower Arranger*. NAFAS sell a series of cards giving basic advice for beginners on most aspects of flower care and arranging.

The Ikebana Trust, 73–75 Kenton Street, London WC1N 1NN
An organization specializing in Japanese arts in this country, especially Japanese flower arranging. The trust arrange their own classes in London, but will put you in touch with an Ikebana class locally. Members are offered a discount on authentic Japanese flower arranging sundries such as vases, available for sale at the Trust. Members receive a circular keeping them in touch with events of interest in the Japanese arts world, as well as advice and background information on Ikebana. The Ikebana Trust will also put people in touch with their local branch of Ikebana International.

The Royal Horticultural Society, Vincent Square, London SW1P 1PE
The gardener's equivalent of NAFAS. Members receive a monthly magazine, *The Garden*, full of information about plants and their cultivation, also useful small ads section where unusual plants may be offered. The RHS run regular shows of horticultural interest at their London headquarters, and occasionally arrange flower arranging demonstrations there too. Members receive free entrance tickets to shows, including the Chelsea Flower Show, and use of the very extensive RHS library.

Publications

Although many excellent books have been written on the subject of flower arranging, some are no longer in print. This list includes only those known to be still available at the time of writing.

ENGLISH-STYLE FLOWER ARRANGING

Nicolette Scourse, *The Victorians and Their Flowers*, Croom Helm

MODERN/ABSTRACT STYLE

Jean Taylor, *Creative Flower Arranging*, Stanley Paul
Marion Aaronson, *Flowers in the Modern Manner*, Grower Books

JAPANESE FLOWER ARRANGING

Takashi Sawano, *Ikebana*, Ward Lock

PRESERVED FLOWER ARRANGING

Maureen Foster, *The Art of Preserved Flower Arranging*, Collins
Maureen Foster, *Creating Pictures with Preserved Flowers*, Collins
Maureen Foster, *Flower Preserving for Beginners*, Collins
Maureen Foster, *Miniature Preserved Flower Arrangements*, Collins
NB. Maureen Foster can supply copies of her earlier books, now out of print: *Making Animal and Bird Collages with Grasses, Leaves, Seedheads and Cones*, £7.95, and *Creating Patterns from Grasses, Seedheads and Cones*, £4.95, both post-free. She also sells her own brand of special flower preserving crystals. For details send stamped addressed envelope to MF Crystals (Dept B8), 77 Bulbridge Road, Wilton, Salisbury, Wilts.

GENERAL

Flora magazine covers all aspects of flower arranging, as well as keeping you in touch with shows and events in the flower world. The small ads are a useful source of out-of-the ordinary flower arranging accessories.

Other information

Details of floristry courses are available from local colleges of further education. For Interflora and similar services available from affiliated florists, see your local yellow pages telephone directory.

Index